Networks, Communication, and Computing Vol. 2

Networks, Communication, and Computing Vol. 2

Editor

Andras Farago

MDPI • Basel • Beijing • Wuhan • Barcelona • Belgrade • Manchester • Tokyo • Cluj • Tianjin

Editor
Andras Farago
The University of Texas at Dallas
USA

Editorial Office
MDPI
St. Alban-Anlage 66
4052 Basel, Switzerland

This is a reprint of articles from the Special Issue published online in the open access journal *Algorithms* (ISSN 1999-4893) (available at: https://www.mdpi.com/si/algorithms/Networks_vol2).

For citation purposes, cite each article independently as indicated on the article page online and as indicated below:

LastName, A.A.; LastName, B.B.; LastName, C.C. Article Title. *Journal Name* **Year**, *Volume Number*, Page Range.

ISBN 978-3-0365-1234-1 (Hbk)
ISBN 978-3-0365-1235-8 (PDF)

© 2021 by the authors. Articles in this book are Open Access and distributed under the Creative Commons Attribution (CC BY) license, which allows users to download, copy and build upon published articles, as long as the author and publisher are properly credited, which ensures maximum dissemination and a wider impact of our publications.

The book as a whole is distributed by MDPI under the terms and conditions of the Creative Commons license CC BY-NC-ND.

Contents

About the Editor vii

Preface to "Networks, Communication, and Computing Vol. 2" ix

Guto Leoni Santos, Patricia Takako Endo, Djamel Sadok and Judith Kelner
When 5G Meets Deep Learning: A Systematic Review
Reprinted from: *Algorithms* **2020**, *13*, 208, doi:10.3390/a13090208 1

András Faragó and Zohre R. Mojaveri
Safe Approximation—An Efficient Solution for a Hard Routing Problem
Reprinted from: *Algorithms* **2021**, *14*, 48, doi:10.3390/a14020048 35

Stephanie Alvarez Fernandez, Marcelo M. Carvalho and Daniel G. Silva
A Hybrid Metaheuristic Algorithm for the Efficient Placement of UAVs
Reprinted from: *Algorithms* **2020**, *13*, 323, doi:10.3390/a13120323 47

Xingxing Xiao and Haining Huang
A Clustering Routing Algorithm Based on Improved Ant Colony Optimization Algorithms for Underwater Wireless Sensor Networks
Reprinted from: *Algorithms* **2020**, *13*, 250, doi:10.3390/a13100250 63

Dehai Zhang, Linan Liu, Cheng Xie, Bing Yang and Qing Liu
Citywide Cellular Traffic Prediction Based on a Hybrid Spatiotemporal Network
Reprinted from: *Algorithms* **2020**, *13*, 20, doi:10.3390/a13010020 81

About the Editor

Andras Farago received the B.Sc., M.Sc. and Ph.D. degrees in electrical engineering from the Technical University of Budapest, Budapest, Hungary, in 1976, 1979 and 1981, respectively. In 1996, he obtained the distinguished title "Doctor of Sciences" from the Hungarian Academy of Sciences. Until 1997, he was faculty member at the Department of Telecommunications and Telematics, Technical University of Budapest. He also worked as a visiting Senior Research Fellow at the University of Massachusetts at Amherst in 1991/92, and spent a sabbatical year at Boston University in 1996. In 1998, he permanently moved to the USA, and became Professor of Computer Science at the University of Texas at Dallas. He is a Senior Member of IEEE, member of ACM, and of the IFIP Working Group 6.3 "Performance of Communication Systems". He serves as Editor for the journal Wireless Networks. His principal research interest is in the analysis, modeling, design, and optimization of networks, as well as the related mathematical background, including algorithms, graph theory and computational complexity. Dr. Farago's research was funded by five grants from the National Science Foundation, and he has authored or co-authored over 250 research papers.

Preface to "Networks, Communication, and Computing Vol. 2"

This book is based on a Special Issue of the *Algorithms* Journal, and it is devoted to the exploration of the many-faceted relationship of networks, communications, and computing, with a particular interest in the interactions among the fields. The included papers explore the current state-of-the-art research on some topics within these areas. Specifically, they cover the following subjects: The article of Guto Leoni Santos, Patricia Takako Endo, Djamel Sadok and Judith Kelner, entitled "When 5G Meets Deep Learning: A Systematic Review" addresses the application of machine learning in fifth generation wireless networks, a promising and heavily researched subject. The paper "Safe Approximation—An Efficient Solution for a Hard Routing Problem" by András Faragó and Zohre R. Mojaveri explores how to solve an algorithmically hard routing problem efficiently via a minor relaxation in the requirements. The article of Stephanie Alvarez Fernandez, Marcelo M. Carvalho and Daniel G. Silva addresses the topic "A Hybrid Metaheuristic Algorithm for the Efficient Placement of Unmanned Arial Vehicles", where optimization and networking meets in a fruitful cooperation. Xingxing Xiao and Haining Huang write about a further encounter between optimization and networking: "A Clustering Routing Algorithm Based on Improved Ant Colony Optimization Algorithms for Underwater Wireless Sensor Networks". Finally, Dehai Zhang, Linan Liu, Cheng Xie, Bing Yang and Qing Liu analyze "Citywide Cellular Traffic Prediction Based on a Hybrid Spatiotemporal Network", presenting another intersection of fifth generation wireless networks and machine learning. All articles demonstrate the trend that networks, communications, and computing have become ubiquitous and inseparable parts of modern technology, and the fruitful interaction among these fields provides a major highway to the future.

Andras Farago
Editor

Article
When 5G Meets Deep Learning: A Systematic Review

Guto Leoni Santos [1], Patricia Takako Endo [2,*], Djamel Sadok [1] and Judith Kelner [1]

[1] Centro de Informática, Universidade Federal de Pernambuco, Recife 50670-901, Brazil; gls4@cin.ufpe.br (G.L.S.); jamel@gprt.ufpe.br (D.S.); jk@gprt.ufpe.br (J.K.)
[2] Programa de Pós-Graduação em Engenharia da Computação, Universidade de Pernambuco, Recife 50100-010, Brazil
* Correspondence: patricia.endo@upe.br

Received: 28 July 2020; Accepted: 20 August 2020; Published: 25 August 2020

Abstract: This last decade, the amount of data exchanged on the Internet increased by over a staggering factor of 100, and is expected to exceed well over the 500 exabytes by 2020. This phenomenon is mainly due to the evolution of high-speed broadband Internet and, more specifically, the popularization and wide spread use of smartphones and associated accessible data plans. Although 4G with its long-term evolution (LTE) technology is seen as a mature technology, there is continual improvement to its radio technology and architecture such as in the scope of the LTE Advanced standard, a major enhancement of LTE. However, for the long run, the next generation of telecommunication (5G) is considered and is gaining considerable momentum from both industry and researchers. In addition, with the deployment of the Internet of Things (IoT) applications, smart cities, vehicular networks, e-health systems, and Industry 4.0, a new plethora of 5G services has emerged with very diverging and technologically challenging design requirements. These include high mobile data volume per area, high number of devices connected per area, high data rates, longer battery life for low-power devices, and reduced end-to-end latency. Several technologies are being developed to meet these new requirements, and each of these technologies brings its own design issues and challenges. In this context, deep learning models could be seen as one of the main tools that can be used to process monitoring data and automate decisions. As these models are able to extract relevant features from raw data (images, texts, and other types of unstructured data), the integration between 5G and DL looks promising and one that requires exploring. As main contribution, this paper presents a systematic review about how DL is being applied to solve some 5G issues. Differently from the current literature, we examine data from the last decade and the works that address diverse 5G specific problems, such as physical medium state estimation, network traffic prediction, user device location prediction, self network management, among others. We also discuss the main research challenges when using deep learning models in 5G scenarios and identify several issues that deserve further consideration.

Keywords: the next generation of telecommunication (5G); deep learning; reinforcement learning; systematic review; cellular networks

1. Introduction

According to Cisco, the global Internet traffic will reach around 30 GB per capita by 2021, where more than 63% of this traffic is generated by wireless and mobile devices [1]. The new generation of mobile communication system (5G) will deal with a massive number of connected devices at base stations, a massive growth in the traffic volume, and a large range of applications with different features and requirements. The heterogeneity of devices and applications makes infrastructure management even more complex. For example, IoT devices require low-power connectivity, trains moving at 300 KM/h need a high-speed mobile connection, users at their home need fiber-like broadband connectivity [2] whereas Industry 4.0 devices require ultra reliable low delay services. Several underlying technologies have been put forward in order to support the above. Examples of these include multiple-input multiple-output (MIMO), antenna beamforming [3], virtualized network functions (VNFs) [4], and the use of tailored and well provisioned network slices [5].

Some data based solutions can be used to manage 5G infrastructures. For instance, analysis of dynamic mobile traffic can be used to predict the user location, which benefits handover mechanisms [6]. Another example is the evaluation of historical physical channel data to predict the channel state information, which is a complex problem to address analytically [7]. Another example is the network slices allocation according to the user requirements, considering network status and the resources available [2]. All these examples are based on data analysis. Some examples are based on historical data analysis, used to predict some behavior, and others are based on the current state of the environment, used to help during decision making process. These type of problems can be addressed through machine learning techniques.

However, the conventional machine learning approaches are limited to process natural data in their raw form [8]. For many decades, constructing a machine learning system or a pattern-recognition system required a considerable expert domain knowledge and careful engineering to design a feature extractor. After this step, the raw data could be converted into a suitable representation to be used as input to the learning system [9].

In order to avoid the effort for creating a feature extractor or suffering possible mistakes in the development process, techniques that automatically discover representations from the raw data were developed. Over recent years, deep learning has outperformed conventional machine learning techniques in several domains such as computer vision, natural language processing, and genomics [10]. According to [9], deep learning methods *"are representation-learning methods with multiple levels of representation, obtained by composing simple but non-linear modules that each transforms the representation at one level (starting with the raw input) into a representation at a higher, slightly more abstract level"*. Therefore, several complex functions can be learned automatically through sufficient and successive transformations from raw data.

Similarly to many application domains, deep learning models can be used to address problems of infrastructure management in 5G networks, such as radio and compute resource allocation, channel state prediction, handover prediction, and so on. This paper presents a systematic review of the literature in order to identify how deep learning has been used to solve problems in 5G environments.

In [11], Ahmed et al. presented some works that applied deep learning and reinforcement learning to address the problem of resource allocation in wireless networks. Many problems and limitations related to resource allocation, such as throughput maximization, interference minimization, and energy efficiency were examined. While the survey presented in [11] focused on the resource allocation problem, in this paper, we offer a more general systematic review spanning the used different deep learning models applied to 5G networks. We also cover other problems present in 5G networks, that demand the use of different deep learning models.

Recently, in [12], Zhang et al. presented an extensive survey about the usage of deep learning in mobile wireless networks. Authors focused on how deep learning was used in mobile networks and potential applications, while identifying the crossover between these areas. Although it is very related to our work, Zhang et al. had a more general focus, addressing problems related to generic wireless networks such as mobility analysis, wireless sensor networks (WSN) localization, WSN data analysis, among others. Our systematic review is focused on 5G networks and their scenarios, applications, and problems. The deep learning models proposed in the analyzed works deal with specific cellular network problems such as channel state information, handover management, spectrum allocation. The scenarios addressed in the works that we select are also related with 5G networks and influence the deep learning-based solution proposed.

Differently, the existing work in the literature, our research identifies some of the main 5G problems addressed by deep learning, highlights the specific types of suitable deep learning models adopted in this context, and delineates the major open challenges when 5G networks meet deep learning solutions.

This paper is structured as follows: Section 2 an overview of the methodology adopted to guide this literature review. The results of the review including descriptive and thematic analysis are presented in Section 3. The paper concludes with a summary of the key findings and contributions of the paper in Section 4.

2. Systematic Review

In this paper, we based our systematic review on the protocol established in [13] with the purpose of finding the works that addressed the usage of deep learning models in the 5G context. We describe the methodology steps in the following subsections.

2.1. Activity 1: Identify the Need for the Review

As discussed previously, both 5G and deep learning are technologies that have received considerable and increasing attention in recent years. Deep learning has become a reality nowadays due to the availability of powerful off-the-shelf hardware and the emergence of new processing processing units such as GPUs. The research community has taken this opportunity to create several public repositories of big data to use in the training and testing of the proposed intelligent models. 5G on the other hand, has a high market appeal as it promises to offer new advanced services that, up until now, no other networking technology was able to offer. 5G importance is boosted by the popularity and ubiquity of mobile, wearable, and IoT devices.

2.2. Activity 2: Define Research Questions

The main goal of this work is to answer the following research questions:

- RQ. 1: What are the main problems deep learning is being used to solve?
- RQ. 2: What are the main learning types used to solve 5G problems (supervised, unsupervised, and reinforcement)?
- RQ. 3: What are the main deep learning techniques used in 5G scenarios?
- RQ. 4: How the data used to train the deep learning models is being gathered or generated?
- RQ. 5: What are the main research outstanding challenges in 5G and deep learning field?

2.3. Activity 3: Define Search String

The search string used to identify relevant literature was: (5G and "deep learning"). It is important to limit the number of strings in order to keep the problem tractable and avoid cognitive overwhelming.

2.4. Activity 4: Define Sources of Research

We considered the following databases as the main sources for our research: IEEE Xplore (http://ieeexplore.ieee.org/Xplore/home.jsp), Science Direct (http://www.sciencedirect.com/), ACM Digital Library (http://dl.acm.org/), and Springer Library (https://link.springer.com/).

2.5. Activity 5: Define Criteria for Inclusion and Exclusion

With the purpose of limiting our scope to our main goal, we considered only papers published in conferences and journals between 2009 and 2019. A selected paper must discuss the use of deep learning in dealing with a 5G technological problem. Note that solutions based on traditional machine learning (shallow learning) approaches were discarded.

2.6. Activity 6: Identify Primary Studies

The search returned 3, 192, 161, and 116 papers (472 in total) from ACM Digital Library, Science Direct, Springer Library, and IEEE Xplore, respectively. We performed this search in early November 2019. After reading all the 472 abstracts and using the cited criteria for inclusion or exclusion, 60 papers were selected for the ultimate evaluation. However, after reading the 60 papers, two papers were discarded because they were considered as being out of scope of this research. Next, two others were eliminated. The first paper was discarded because it was incomplete, and the second one was removed due presenting several inconsistencies in its results. Therefore, a total of 56 papers were selected for the for ultimate data extraction and evaluation (see Table A1 in Appendix A).

2.7. Activity 7: Extract Relevant Information

After reading the 56 papers identified in Activity 6, the relevant information was extracted as it attempted to answer some of the research questions presented in the Activity 2.

2.8. Activity 8: Present an Overview of the Studies

An overview of all works will be presented in this activity (see Section 3), in order to classify and clarify the conducted works according to our research questions presented in Activity 2.

2.9. Activity 9: Present the Results of the Research Questions

Finally, an overview of the studies in deep learning as it is applied to 5G is produced. It will discuss our findings and address our research questions stated in Activity 2 (see Section 3).

3. Results

In this section, we present our answers for the research question formulated previously.

3.1. What are the Main Problems Deep Learning Is Being Used to Solve?

In order to answer RQ. 1, this subsection presents an overview of the papers found in the systematic review. We separated the papers according to the problem addressed as shown in Figure 1. The identified problems can be categorized in three main layers: physical medium, network, and application.

At the physical level of the OSI reference model, we detected papers that addressed problems related to channel state information (CSI) estimation, coding/decoding scheme representation, fault detection, device prediction location, self interference, beamforming definition, radio frequency characterization, multi user detection, and radio parameter definition. At the network level, the works addressed traffic prediction through deep learning models and anomaly detection. Research on resource allocation can be related to the physical or network level. Finally, at the application level, existing works proposed deep learning-based solutions for application characterization.

In the following subsections, we will describe the problems solved by deep learning models; further details about the learning and the deep learning types used in the models will be presented in Sections 3.2 and 3.3, respectively.

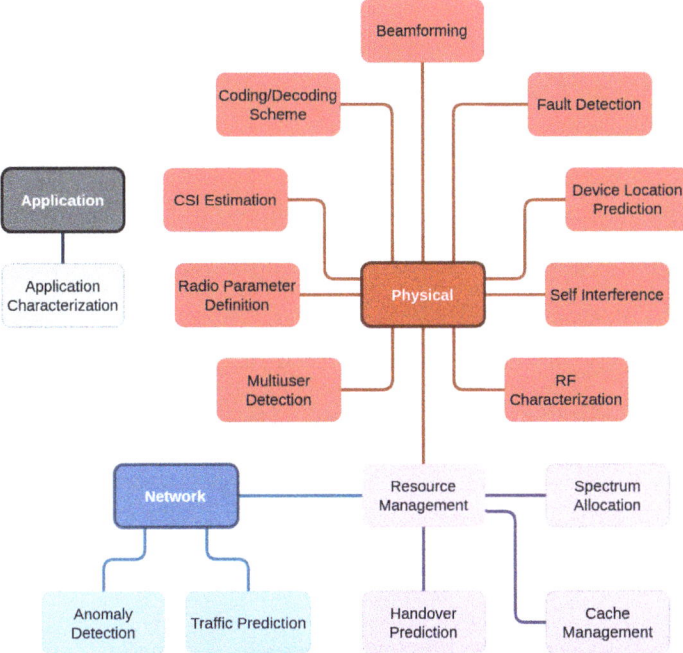

Figure 1. The problems related to 5G addressed in the works examined.

3.1.1. Channel State Information Estimation

CSI estimation is a common problem in wireless communication systems. It refers to the channel properties of a communication link [7]. In a simplified way, these properties describe how the signal will propagate from the transmitter to the receiver. Based on the CSI, the transmission can be adapted according to the current channel conditions, in order to improve the whole communication. CSI is an important factor in determining radio resource allocation, the type of modulation and coding schemes to use, etc.

Traditional CSI estimation techniques usually require high computation capability [14]. In addition, these techniques may not be suitable for 5G scenarios due to the complexity of the new scenarios and the presence of different technologies (e.g., massive MIMO, orthogonal frequency division multiplexing (OFDM), and millimeter-Wave), that impact the physical medium conditions [7]. Therefore, several authors have used deep learning models for CSI estimation. In our systematic review, we came across five papers related to CSI estimation with deep learning.

Three works proposed a deep learning-based solution focused on MIMO systems [15–17]. In MIMO systems both transmitter and receiver are equipped with an array of antennas. This is a very important technology for 5G, offering multiple orders of spectral and energy efficiency gains in comparison to LTE technologies [18]. Note that LTE uses MIMO but 5G takes this technology a notch further as it adopts massive antenna configurations in what is known as massive MIMO.

In [15], the authors adopted deep learning for decision-directed for channel estimation (DD-CE) in MIMO systems, to avoid the Doppler rate estimation. Authors considered vehicular channels, where the Doppler rate varies from one packet to another, making the CSI estimation difficult. Therefore, the deep learning model was used to learn and estimate the MIMO fading channels over different Doppler rates.

In [16], the authors proposed a combination of deep learning and superimposed code (SC) techniques for channel state CSI feedback. The main goal is to estimate downlink CSI and detect user data in the base stations.

In [17], Jiang et al. presented some evaluations for CSI estimation using deep learning models in three use cases. The first one focused on MIMO with multi users where the angular power spectrum (APS) information is estimated using deep learning models; and the two other scenarios were (a) static CSI estimation framework based on deep learning; and (b) a variant of the first scheme, but considering time variation, i.e., a deep learning model is proposed to estimate the CSI through time.

In [7], Luo et al. proposed an online CSI prediction taking into account relevant features that affect the CSI of a radio link, such as frequency band, user location, time, temperature, humidity, and weather.

In [19], a residual network was proposed for CSI estimation in filter bank multicarrier (FBMC) systems. The traditional CSI estimation and equalization and demapping module are replaced by deep learning model.

3.1.2. Coding/Decoding Scheme Representation

The generation of the information at the source and the reconstruction of such information at the receiver makes up the coding and decoding processes, respectively. However, due to the unstable nature of the channels, some disturbances and noise in the signal can cause data corruption [20]. Considering the 5G networks, where new technologies, such as MIMO, non-orthogonal multiple access (NOMA), mmWave will be deployed, the coding/decoding schemes must be adapted to work properly. These schemes need to characterize several phenomena that can impact the data transmission, such as signal diffraction, fading, path loss, and scattering.

We identified a total of seven works that addressed the coding/decoding schemes using deep learning models.

Three of these considered NOMA technology using deep learning models. In [21], the authors proposed a deep learning-based solution to parameterize the bit-to-symbol mapping and multi-user detection. Recall that as we are using non orthogonal modulation, multi-user detection becomes a cumbersome issue. In [22], the authors proposed a deep learning model to learn the coding/decoding process of MIMO-NOMA system in order to minimize the total mean square error of the users signals. In [23], the authors proposed a deep learning model to be used in sparse code multiple access (SCMA) system, which is a promising code-based NOMA technique, with the goal to minimize the bit error rate.

The authors in [24] considered multiuser single-input multiple-output (MU-SIMO) systems. A simple deep learning model was considered for joint multi user waveform design at the transmitter side, and non coherent signal detection at the receiver side. The main goal was to reduce the difference between the transmitted and received signals.

In [25], Kim et al. proposed a novel peak-to-average power ratio (PAPR) reduction scheme using deep learning of OFDM systems. The presence of large PAPR values is harmful to battery life as high peaks tend to draw high levels of energy from sometimes energy limited devices. The model proposed map and demap symbols on each subcarrier adaptively and both bit error rate (BER) and the PAPR of the OFDM system could be jointly minimized.

In [26], a deep learning based unified polar-low-density parity-check (LDPC) is proposed. The deep learning model was created to receive the observed symbols and an additional information introduced by the authors called "indicator section", and to output the signal decoded.

In [27], a coding mechanism under low latency constraints based on deep learning was proposed. The idea was to create a robust and adaptable mechanism for generic codes for future communications.

3.1.3. Fault Detection

Fault detection systems are very important to achieving ultra-reliable low latency communication (URLLC). For example, mission-critical industrial automation applications is a type of application that demands stringent timing and reliability guarantees for data collection, transmission, and processing [28]. Identifying faults is crucial to ensure low latency (since damaged equipment may increase the time transmission) and reliable communication (since point of failure may reduce the overall network performance). However, due to the device heterogeneity of 5G networks, identifying faults is a complex task that requires sophisticated techniques in order to automate such task.

In this systematic review, we found two papers that addressed fault detection in 5G scenarios using deep learning models.

In [29], a deep-learning-based schema was proposed to detect and locate antenna faults in mmWave systems. Firstly, the scheme detects the faults (using a simple neural network with a low cost), and then it locates where the fault occurred. Since the second step is a more complex task due to the high number of antennas present in a mmWave system, a more complex neural network was proposed.

In [30], Yu et al. covered fronthaul network faults. The model was designed to locate single-link faults in 5G optical fronthaul networks. The proposed model was able to identify faults and false alarms among alarm information considering single-link connections.

3.1.4. Device Location Prediction

Unlike traditional networks, in telecommunication networks, the nodes are characterized by a high mobility; and determining or estimating their mobility behavior is a complex task. Device location prediction has many applications, such as location-based services, mobile access control, mobile multimedia quality of service (QoS) provision, as well as the resource management for mobile computation and storage [31].

Considering urban scenarios, it is known that movement of people has a high degree of repetition, because they visit regular places in the city such as their own homes and places of work. These patterns can help to build services for specific places in order to increase user experience [32]. In addition, more detailed information about human mobility across the city can be collected using smartphones [33]. This information (combined with other data sources) can be used as input for models to estimate the device and consequently user location with high accuracy.

In this systematic review, three articles presented models to deal with device location prediction. Two works focused on device location prediction in mmWave systems [34,35]. In these systems, predicting the device location is a complex task due to the radiation reflected on most visible objects, which creates a rich multi path (interference) environment. In [34], a deep learning model was used to predict user location based on the radiation sent by the obstacles encountered. These carry latent information regarding their relative positions; while in [35], fingerprint historical data was used to estimate the device location over beamformed fingerprints.

In [36], the authors proposed a deep learning model to predict the device location in ultra-dense networks. Predicting the device location in this scenario is important because the deployment of small cells inevitably leads to more frequent handovers, making the mobility process more challenging. The model was used to predict user mobility and anticipate the handover preparation. The model was designed to estimate the future position of an user based on her/his historical data. If a handover is estimated as being eminent, deep learning model was able to determine the best base station to receive the user.

3.1.5. Anomaly Detection

Future 5G networks will lead with different types of devices over heterogeneous wireless networks with higher data rates, lower latency and lower power consumption. Autonomous management mechanisms will be needed to reduce the control and monitoring of these complex networks [37].

Anomaly detection systems are important to identify malicious network flows that may impact users and the network performance. However, developing these systems remains a considerable challenge due to the large data volume generated in 5G systems [38,39].

Four articles addressing the anomaly detection problem using deep learning in 5G were identified in this systematic review. In [38,40], the authors deal with cyber security defense systems in 5G networks, proposing the use of deep learning models that are capable of extracting features from network flows and the quick identification of cyber threats.

In [10,41], the authors proposed a deep learning-based solution to detect anomalies in the network traffic, considering two types of behavior as network anomalies: sleeping cells and soared traffic. Sleeping cells can happen due to failures in the antenna hardware or random access channel (RACH) failures due to RACH misconfiguration, while soared traffic can result in network congestion, where traffic increases but with relatively smaller throughput to satisfy the users' demand. Recall that RACH is the channel responsible for giving users radio resources so when RACH is not working properly we effectively have a sleepy cell with no transmission activity taking place.

3.1.6. Traffic Prediction

It is expected that Internet traffic will grow tenfold by 2027. This acts as a crucial anchor to create the new generation of cellular network architecture [42]. Predicting traffic for the next day, hour, or even the next minute can be used to optimize the available system resources, for example by reducing the energy consumption, applying opportunistic scheduling, or preventing problems in the infrastructure [42].

In this systematic review, we found eight works that addressed traffic prediction using deep learning.

The works presented in [43,44] proposed a deep learning-based solution to predict traffic for network slicing mechanisms. Note that 5G relies on the use of network slicing in order to accommodate different services and tenants while virtually isolating them. In [43], a proactive network slice mechanism was proposed and a deep learning model was used to predict the traffic with high accuracy. In [44], a mechanism named DeepCog was proposed with a similar purpose. DeepCog can forecast the capacity needed to allocate future traffic demands in network slices while minimizing service request violations and resource overprovisioning.

Three works considered both temporal and spatial dependence of cell traffic. In [6], the authors proposed a deep learning model to predict citywide traffic. The proposed model was able to capture the spatial dependency and two temporal dependencies: closeness and period. In [45], the authors proposed different deep learning models for mobile Internet traffic prediction. The authors used the different models to consider spatial and temporal aspects of the traffic. The maximum, average, and minimum traffic were predicted for the proposed models. In [46], the authors proposed a deep learning-based solution to allocate remote radio heads (RRHs) into baseband unit (BBU) pools in a cloud radio access network (C-RAN) architecture. The deep learning model was used to predict traffic demand of the RRHs considering the spatial and temporal aspects. The prediction was used to create RRH clusters and map them to BBU pools in order to maximize the average BBU capacity utility and minimize the overall deployment cost.

In [47], the authors considered traffic prediction in ultra-dense networks, which is a complicated scenario due to the presence of beamforming and massive MIMO technologies. A deep learning model was used to predict the traffic in order to detect if a congestion will take place and then take decisions to avoid/alleviate such congestion.

In [48], the authors addressed the benefits of cache offloading in small base stations considering the mobile edge computing (MEC). The offloading decision is based on the users' data rate, where the users with low data rates are offloaded first. Consequently, the authors proposed a deep learning model to predict the traffic data rate of the users in order to have a guide for the scheduling offloading mechanism.

3.1.7. Handover Prediction

The handover process ensures continuous data transfer when users are on the move between call towers. For that, the mobile management entity (MME) must update the base stations where the users are connected. This procedure is known as location update. The handover delay is one of the main problems in wireless networks [49]. Conventionally, a handover is carried out based on a predefined threshold of the Reference Signal Receiver Power (RSRP), the Reference Signal Receiver Quality (RSRQ), among other signal strength parameters [50]. Predicting the handover based on the nearby stations' parameters can be a fruitful strategy to avoid handover errors, temporary disconnections and improve user experience [49].

In this systematic review, we located two papers that addressed handover prediction. In [51], Khunteta et al. proposed a deep learning model to avoid handover failures. For that, the deep learning model was trained to detect if the handover will fail or be successful based on the historical signal condition data.

In [52], the handover prediction was tested to provide uninterrupted access to wireless services without compromising the expected QoS. The authors proposed both analytical and deep learning-based approaches to predict handover events in order to reduce the holistic cost.

3.1.8. Cache Optimization

In the last decade, multimedia data became dominant in mobile data traffic. This raised additional challenges in transporting the big volume of data from the content providers to the end users with high-rates and low latency. The main bottleneck point is the severe traffic congestion observed in the backhaul links, specially in 5G scenarios, where several small base stations will be scattered [53]. To mitigate this issue, the most popular content can be stored (cached) at the edge of the network (e.g., in the base stations) in order to free backhaul link usage [54]. However, finding the best strategy for the cache placement is a challenge. The best content to cache and the best location for storing this content are both decisions that can impact the cache scheme performance.

Two works addressed the cache placement problem in 5G environments using deep learning models. In [55], authors proposed a collaborative cache mechanism in multiple RRHs to multiple BBUs based on reinforcement learning. This approach was used because rule-based and metaheuristics methods suffer some limitations and fail to consider all environmental factors. Therefore, by using reinforcement learning, the best cache strategy can be selected in order to reduce the transmission latency from the remote cloud and the traffic load of backhaul.

In [56], the authors considered ultra-dense heterogeneous networks where the content cache is performed at small base stations. The goal is to minimize energy consumption and reduce the transmission delay, optimizing the whole cache placement process. Instead of using traditional optimization algorithms, a deep learning model was trained to learn the best cache strategy. This model reduces the computational complexity achieving a real time optimization.

3.1.9. Resource Allocation/Management

As the numbers of users, services, and resources increase, the management and orchestration complexity of resources also increase. The efficient usage of resources can be translated into cost reduction and avoid over/under resource dimensioning. Fortunately, under such a very dynamic and complex network environment, recent achievements in machine learning that interact with surrounding environments can provide effective way to address these problems [57].

Four papers addressed resource allocation in network slices using solutions based on deep learning [5,57–59]. A network slice is a very important technology for 5G since it will allow a network operator to offer a diverse set of tailored and isolated services over a shared physical infrastructure.

A deep learning-based solution was proposed in [58] to allocate slices in 5G networks. The authors proposed a metric called REVA that measures the amount of Physical Resource Blocks (PRBs) available to active bearers for each network slice, and a deep learning model was proposed to predict such metric.

Yan et al. proposed a framework that combined deep learning and reinforcement learning to resource scheduling and allocation [57]. The main goal was to minimize resource consumption at the same time guaranteeing the required performance isolation degree by a network slice. In [5], the authors proposed a framework for resource allocation in network slices and a deep learning model was used to predict the network status based on historical data. In [59], a model was proposed to predict the medium usage for network slices in 5G environments while meeting service level agreement (SLA) requirements.

Three papers proposed deep learning-based solutions to optimize the energy consumption in 5G networks [60–63]. The works proposed by [60,61] focused on NOMA systems. A framework was proposed in [60] to optimize energy consumption. A deep learning model is part of the framework and was used to map the input parameters (channel coefficients, the user demands, user power, and the transmission deadline) into an optimal scheduling scheme. In [61], a similar strategy was used, where a deep learning model was used to find the approximated optimal joint resource allocation strategy to minimize energy consumption. In [62], a deep learning model was used in the MME for user association taking into account the behavior of access points in the offloading scheme. In [63], the authors proposed a deep learning model to allocate carriers in multi-carrier power amplifier (MCPA) dynamically, taking into account the energy efficiency. The main idea was to minimize the total power consumption while finding the optimal carrier to MPCA allocation. To solve this problem, two approaches were used: convex relaxation and deep learning. The deep learning model was used to approximate the power consumption function formulated in the optimization problem, since it is a non-convex and non-continuous function.

In [64], the authors proposed a deep learning-based solution for downlink coordinated multi-point (CoMP) in 5G. The model receives physical layer measurements from the user equipment and "formulates a modified CoMP trigger function to enhance the downlink capacity" [64]. The output of the model is the decision to enable/disable the CoMP mechanism.

In [65], the authors proposed a deep learning model for smart communication systems with high density D2D mmWave environments using beamforming. The model selects the best relay node taking into account multiple reliability metrics in order to maximize the average system throughput. The authors in [11] also proposed a deep learning-based solution to maximize the network throughput considering resource allocation in multi-cell networks. A deep learning model was proposed to predict the resource allocation solution (taking as input the channel quality indicator and user location) without intensive computations.

3.1.10. Application Characterization

In cellular networks, self-organizing networks (SON) is a technology designed to plan, deploy, operate, and optimize mobile radio access networks in a simple, fast, and automated way. SON is a key technology for future cellular networks due to the potential of saving capital expenditure (CAPEX) and operational expenditure (OPEX). However, SON is not only about network performance but also QoS. A better planning of network resources can be translated into a better service quality and increasing revenues.

The authors in [66,67] presented a framework for self-optimization in 5G networks called APP-SON. It was designed to optimize some target network key performance indicators (KPIs) based on the mobile applications characteristics, by identifying similar application features and creating clusters using the Hungarian Algorithm Assisted Clustering (HAAC). The homogeneous application characteristics of cells in a cluster are identified to prioritize target network KPIs in order to improve user quality of experience (QoE). This is achieved through cell engineering parameters adjustments. The deep learning model was used to establish cause effect between the cell engineering parameters and the network KPIs. For instance, Video application KPIs can be used to detect that this type of traffic occupies more than 90% of the total traffic, and thus adjust the cell engineering parameters to give priority to video traffic.

3.1.11. Other Problems

Some papers addressed problems which are not related to the ones previously listed. Thus, we will describe them separately.

The work presented in [68] applied a deep learning model to a massive MIMO system to solve the pilot contamination problem [69]. The authors highlighted that conventional approaches of pilot assignment are based on heuristics that are difficult to deploy in a real system due to high complexity. The model was used to learn the relationship between the users' location and the near-optimal pilot assignment with low computational complexity, and consequently could be used in real MIMO scenarios.

The self-interference problem was addressed in [70]. A digital cancellation scheme based on deep learning was proposed for full-duplex systems. The proposed model was able to discover the relationship between the signal sent through the channel and the self-interference signal received. The authors evaluated how the joint effects of non-linear distortion and linear multi-path channel impact the performance of digital cancellation using the deep learning model.

The authors in [71] represented the characterization of radio frequency (RF) power amplifiers (PAs) using deep learning. While in previous works they have considered only linear aspects of PA, the authors included non-linear aspects of PA taking into account memory aspects of deep learning models in [71]. They defined the map between the digital base station stimulus and the response of PA as a non-linear function. However, the conventional methods to solve this function require a designer to extract the interest parameters for each input (base station stimulus) manually. As a result, a deep learning model was proposed to represent this function, extracting the parameters automatically from measured base station stimulus and giving as output the PA response.

In [2], reinforcement learning was used to learn the optimal physical-layer control parameters of different scenarios. Authors proposed a self-driving radio, which learns the near-optimal control algorithm while taking int account the high-level design specifications provided by the network designer. A deep learning model was proposed to map the network specifications into physical-layer control instructions. This model was then used in the reinforcement learning algorithm to take decisions according to feedback from the environment.

In [72], the spectrum auction problem was addressed using deep learning. The idea was to allocate spectrum among unlicensed users taking into account the interests of the channel for the auction, and the interference suffered during communication as well as economic capability. A deep learning model was proposed for spectrum auction, and it receives as input three factors: the interference, experience, and economic ability; and gives as output a number between zero and one that determines whether the channel will be allocated for a user or not.

In [73], path scheduling in a multi path scenario was addressed using reinforcement learning. In these systems, the traffic is distributed across the different paths according to policies, packet traffic classes, and the performance of the available paths. Thus, reinforcement learning was used to learn from the network the best approach for scheduling packets across the different paths.

The security aspect of cooperative NOMA systems was considered in [74]. In cooperative NOMA, the user with a better channel condition acts as a relay between the source and a user experiencing poor channel conditions (user receiver). The security may be compromised in the presence of an eavesdropper in the network. Therefore, a deep learning model was proposed to find the optimal power allocation factor of a receiver in a communication system has the presence of an eavesdropper node.

The model input data are the channel realization while the output are the power allocation factor of the user with poor channel conditions.

In [75], authors considered the propagation prediction using deep learning models. Predicting the propagation characteristics accurately is needed for optimum cell design. Thus, the authors proposed a deep learning model to learn propagation loss from the map of a geographical area with high accuracy.

The authors in [76] considered the multiuser detection problem in an SCMA system. A deep learning model was used to mimic the message passing algorithm (MPA), which is the most popular approach to implement multiuser detection with low complexity. The deep learning model was designed to estimate the probability that a user is assigned into a resource block from a pool of resource blocks, taken the signal sent by the users as input.

In [3], an intelligent beamforming technique based on MIMO technology was proposed using reinforcement learning. The proposal builds a self-learning system to determine the phase shift and the amplitude of each antenna. The reinforcement learning algorithm can adapt the signal concentration based on the number of users located in a given area. If there are many users in a given small area, the solution may produce a more targeted signal for users located at that area. However, if users are spread out over a wide area, a signal with wide coverage will be sent to cover the entire area.

In [77], Tsai et al. proposed a reinforcement learning-based solution in order to choose the best configuration of uplink and downlink channels in dynamic time-division duplexing (TDD) systems. The main goal was to optimize the mean opinion score (MOS), which is a QoE metric. This metric has a direct relationship with the system throughput. The optimization problem was formulated as one that maximizes the MOS of the system by allocating uplink and downlik traffic for the time frames. Thus, a set of downlink and uplink configurations was defined by the authors and, for each frame, these configurations are chosen for each base station.

3.2. What Are the Main Types of Learning Techniques Used to Solve 5G Problems?

The works captured in this systematic review used three different learning techniques, as shown in Figure 2. The majority of the these works used supervised learning (fifty articles), followed by reinforcement learning (seven articles), and unsupervised learning (four articles only).

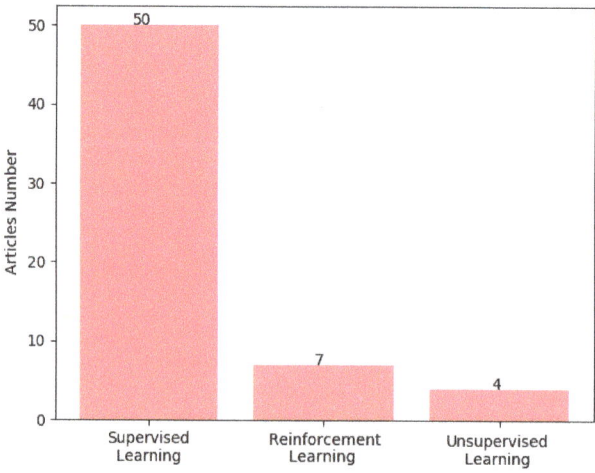

Figure 2. Most common learning type used in the deep learning models for 5G.

3.2.1. Supervised Learning

Although it is hard to find labeled datasets in 5G scenarios, most of the papers used the supervised learning approach. This approach is widely used for classification tasks (such as [78–81]) and regression problems (such as [82–85]), what are the most common problems addressed in the works found in this systematic review.

We classified the 50 articles that used supervised learning between classification and regression problems as shown in Table 1. We can see that 32 articles addressed classification problems in 5G scenarios whereas 19 articles dealt with regression models.

Table 1. Articles that used supervised learning in their deep learning models.

Problem Type	Number of Articles	References
Classification	32	[2,10,11,16,17,19,21–23,26,27,29,30,34,38,40,41,52,56,60–66,68,71,72,74–76]
Regression	19	[5–7,15,17,35,36,43–48,51,57–59,67,70]

3.2.2. Reinforcement Learning

Reinforcement learning has received a lot of attention in the last years. This paradigm is based on trial and error, where software agents learn a behavior that optimizes the reward observing the consequences of their actions [86]. The works we reviewed addressed different problems while taking into account context information and solving optimization problems. For instance, authors in [3] used reinforcement learning to determine phase shift and amplitude of each antenna element with the purpose to optimize the aggregated throughput of the antennas. In [62], authors used reinforcement learning to improve the URLLC energy efficiency and delay tolerant services through resource allocation. In [73], the authors also considered a URLLC service but this time they worked on optimizing packet scheduling of a multipath protocol using reinforcement learning. In [57], the authors adopted reinforcement learning for network slicing in RAN in an attempt to optimize resource utilization. To handle the cache allocation problem in multiple RRHs and multiple BBU pools, the authors in [55] used reinforcement learning to maximize the cache hit rate and maximize the cache capacity. In [77], reinforcement learning was used to configure indoor small cell networks in order to optimize opinion score (MOS) and user QoE. Finally, in [2], reinforcement learning was used to select radio parameters and optimize different metrics according with the scenario addressed.

3.2.3. Unsupervised Learning

We examined four articles that used unsupervised learning to train the models proposed. In [61], the authors proposed a hybrid approach with both supervised and unsupervised learning to train the model with the purpose to determine an approximate solution for optimal joint resource allocation strategy and energy consumption. The authors in [30] also used a hybrid learning approach, combining supervised and unsupervised learning to train the model in order to identify faults and false alarms among alarm information considering single link connections. In [25], the authors trained a deep learning model through unsupervised learning to map constellation mapping and demapping of symbols on each subcarrier in an OFDM system, while minimizing the BER. In [24], an unsupervised deep learning model was proposed to represent a MU-SIMO system. Its main purpose was to reduce the difference between the signal transmitted and the signal received.

3.3. What Are the Main Deep Learning Techniques Used in 5G Scenarios?

Figure 3 shows the common deep learning techniques used to address 5G problems in the literature. Traditional neural networks with fully connected layers is the deep learning technique that most appears in the works (reaching 24 articles), followed by long short-term memory (LSTM) (with 14 articles), and convolutional neural network (CNN) (adopted by only 9 articles).

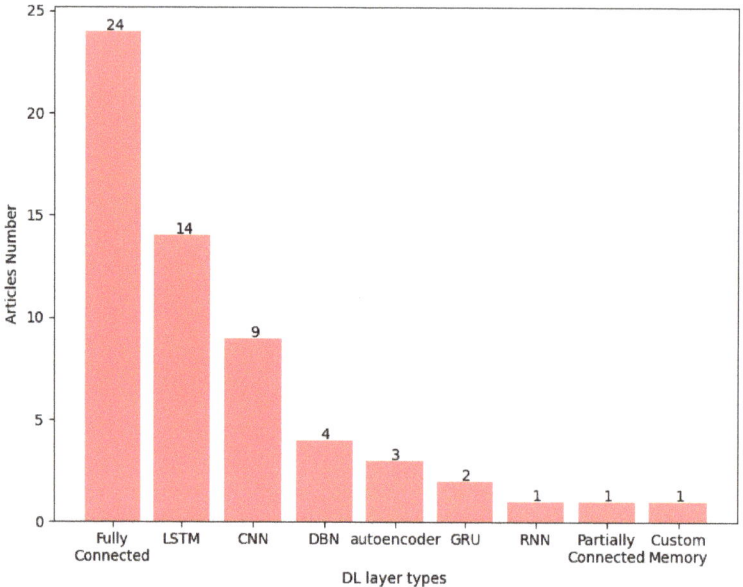

Figure 3. Most common deep learning techniques for 5G.

3.3.1. Fully Connected Models

Most of the works that used fully connected layers addressed problems related to the physical medium in 5G systems [2,11,15–17,21,22,24,26,56,60,62–65,68,72,74,76]. This can be justified because physical information usually can be structured (e.g., CSI, channel quality indicator (CQI), radio condition information, etc.). In addition, these works did not consider more complex data, such as historical information. It is understandable that the 5G physical layer receives such attention. It is the scene of a number of new technologies such as mmWave, MIMO and antenna beamforming. These are very challenging technologies that require real time fine tuning.

However, although fully connected layers were not designed to deal with sequential data, some works found in this systematic review proposed models based on time series. In [10,41], the authors considered real data of cellular networks such as Internet usage, SMS, and calls. Although the dataset has spatio-temporal characteristics, the authors extracted features to compose a new input for the deep learning model. In [52], the authors proposed a fully connected model to deal with user coordinate location data. In this work both fully connected and LSTM models were proposed for comparison and the temporal aspect of dataset was maintained. In [66], the authors adopted a dataset composed of historical data records for urban and rural areas. Unfortunately, the paper did not provide more details about the data used, but a deep learning model composed of fully connected layers was used to process this data.

In [73], a fully connected model was used with a reinforcement learning algorithm. In this work, the open source public Mininet simulator was used to create a network topology (the environment) in order to train the agent. Subsequently, the deep learning model was used to chose the best action according with the environment.

3.3.2. Recurrent Neural Networks

As highlighted in [9], a recurrent neural network (RNN) is able to deal with sequential data, such as time series, speech and language. It is due to its capacity for, given an element in a sequence, storing information of past elements. Therefore, one work used RNN [17] and several others used RNN variations (such as LSTM [87–90]) to deal with sequential data.

In [70], Zhang et al. proposed a digital cancellation scheme to eliminate linear and non-linear interference based on deep learning. The deep learning model receives a signal and the custom loss function represents the residual interference between the real and estimated self-interference signal. This model was based on RNN but with a custom memory unit.

In [17], authors used data from channel estimations using the ray tracing propagation software. The data was processed using traditional RNN layers to capture the time-varying nature of CSI. Similarly, several works adopted deep learning models with LSTM layers. This can be justified as LSTM is widely used in the literature to process sequential data.

The authors in [45,46] used the same dataset to train their models (Telecom Italia, see the Section 3.4). In [46], a multivariate LSTM model was proposed to learn the temporal and spatial correlation among the base station traffic and make an accurate forecast. In [45], an LSTM model was proposed to extract temporal features of mobile Internet traffic and predict Internet flows for cellular networks.

In [52], an LSTM model was suggested to deal with another open dataset in order to predict handover. The dataset is composed of historical location of the users, and the model exploits the long-term dependencies and temporal correlation of data.

In [48], the authors proposed an LSTM model for handling historical data of traffic volume. The model was constructed to predict real time traffic of base stations in order to give relevant information to increase the accuracy of the offloading scheme proposed.

In [47], Zhou et al. also proposed an LSTM model to predict traffic in base stations in order to avoid flow congestion in 5G ultra dense networks. Uplink and downlink flows data were considered as input for the model. With the predicted data, it is possible to allocate more resources for uplink or downlink channels accordingly.

In [7], an LSTM model was proposed to make online CSI prediction. The model explored the temporal dependency of historical data of frequency band, location, time, temperature, humidity, and weather. The dataset was measured through experiments within a testbed.

In [58], a variation of LSTM called X-LSTM was proposed in order to predict a metric called REVA, which measures the amount of PRBs available in a network slice. X-LSTM is based on X-11, which is an interative process that decomposes the data into seasonal patterns. X-LSTM uses different LSTM models to evaluate different time scales of data. *"It filters out higher order temporal patterns and uses the residual to make additional predictions on data with a shorter time scale"* [58]. The input data of the model is the historical data of PRB measured through a testbed, where the REVA metric was calculated.

In [71], the authors represented the memory aspect PA using a biLSTM model. The authors established a bridge between the theoretical formalism of PA behavior and the characteristic of biLSTM models to consider both forward an backward temporal aspect of the input data (baseband measurements using a testbed).

In [35,36,51,59], the authors used LSTM to deal with sequential data generated through simulation. In [59], the LSTM model was used to predict if a new network slice can be allocated given the sequential data of allocated resources and channel conditions. In [51], the LSTM model was used to evaluate historical signal condition in order to classify event in either handover fail or success in advance. In [36], the developed LSTM model was applied to learn the users mobility pattern in order to predict their movement trends in the future based on historical trajectories. In [35], the authors used LSTM to predict position of users based on historical beamformed fingerprint data (considering the presence o buildings in a scenario generated through simulations).

The work presented in [26] proposed an LSTM model to represent the coding/decoding schema considering a hybrid approach to support polar codes. Unfortunately, the authors did not describe the data used to train their model.

In [27,43], gated recurrent unit (GRU) layers are considered to deal with sequential data. In [43], real ISP data is used to train the model. The authors used a testbed to create the dataset composed of GPON (ZTE C320) to demonstrate the fronthaul, while midhaul and backhaul are enabled by the MPLS feature of SDN switches. Details about the dataset used in [27] are not provided.

3.3.3. CNN

CNN models are created to deal with data that come from multiple arrays or multivariate arrays and extract relevant features from them. In other words, the convolution layer is applied to process data with different dimensionality: 1D for signals and sequences, 2D for images or audio spectrograms, and 3D for video or volumetric images [9]. As a result, this layer was typically used to deal with several types of data in the works found in this systematic review.

The works in [29,34,35,75], presented the input data for the CNN models as an image form in order to take advantage of the natural features of the convolutions applied by the CNN layers. Both temporal and geographical aspects were considered in the works presented in [6,44,45]. These are relevant plans since the metrics have different behavior according to the time of the day and the base station location. As a result, these works used CNN to take into consideration temporal and space aspects at the same time and extract relevant joint patterns. The works presented in [7] used CNN models and considered several aspects that affect the CSI as input for the models such as frequency band, location, time, temperature, humidity, and weather. The authors considered 1D and 2D convolutions in order to extract frequency representative vector from CSI information.

A separate work used a special architecture of CNN called ResNet [19]. This architecture was proposed to solve the notorious problem of a vanishing/exploding gradient. The main difference offered by the ResNet architecture is that a shortcut connection is added every two or three layers in order to skip the connections and reuse activation from a previous layer until the adjacent layer learns its weights. This architecture was used to process modulated frequency-domain sequence data for the purpose of channel estimation.

In addition to the LSTM and CNN models, the authors proposed a model named a temporal convolutional network (TCN) in [35]. Unlike the other models, the TCN architecture considers the temporal dependency in a more accurate way. The interested reader may find out more detailed information TCN by consulting [91].

In [26], besides describing a fully connected layers and an LSTM models, the authors also proposed a CNN model for use with LSTM to represent the coding/decoding schema as convolution functions.

3.3.4. DBN

Deep belief networks (DBNs) are attractive for problems with few labeled data and a large amount of unlabeled ones. This is mainly due to the fact that during the training process, unlabeled data are used for training the model and the labeled data are used for fine-tuning the entire network [92]. Therefore, this deep learning technique combines both supervised and unsupervised learning during the training process.

For instance, the works presented in [38,40] used a dataset composed of several network flows of computers infected with botnets. The DBN model was used to detect traffic anomalies.

Similarly, in [61], the authors proposed a DBN model where the dataset used consisted of the channel coefficients and the respective optimal downlink resource allocation solution.

In [30], another DBN model was trained using a hybrid approach (supervised and unsupervised) for fault location on optical fronthalls. The dataset used was taken from a real management system of a network operator, and consists of link faults events.

3.3.5. Autoencoder

Autoencoders networks can be trained to reconstruct their input as the output [8]. Internally, these networks have a hidden layer that describes the internal representation of input. This representation can be used to construct back the input, that is the output of these networks. Therefore, the works used autoencoder architecture to encode and decode signal transmitted through the physical medium. We found three works in this systematic review that used an autoencoder architecture [23,25,27].

3.3.6. Combining Models

Most of the examined works make use of only one deep learning technique, but we have seen that there are eight works that considered more than one technique and provided a combination with other(s).

For instance, the authors in [52] proposed the joint use of an LSTM and a fully connected model. The research in [57] combined LSTM with reinforcement learning, [75] proposed a solution combining a CNN model with a fully connected model, [62,73] combined a fully connected model with reinforcement learning. Finally a combination of LSTM with CNN was proposed in [7,45]. A hybrid model, generative adversarial network (GAN), combining both LSTM and CNN layers was adopted in [5].

Next we discuss how the datasets were used to train these deep learning models.

3.4. How the Data Used to Train the Deep Learning Models Was Gathered/Generated?

Deep learning models (both supervised and unsupervised) require datasets for their training and testing. However, acquiring a good dataset, in some cases, remains a considerable challenge.

The works we reviewed either used different datasets or created their own data using different techniques, as shown in the Table 2.

Table 2. Data source.

Data Source	Number of Articles	References
Generated through simulation	24	[2,15–17,25,34–36,47,51,55–57,59–64,68,72,73,75,77]
Real data (generated using prototypes or public dataset)	18	[5–7,10,30,38,40,41,43–46,48,52,58,66,67,71]
Synthetic (generated randomly)	4	[11,19,74,76]
Not described (the work did not provide information about the dataset used)	10	[3,21–24,26,27,29,65,70]

Most of works (more precisely 24 of them) used simulation to generate their dataset. This is often justified as the authors are unable to a suitable variety of available datasets focused on 5G, since this is a novel technology and is being slowly deployed since 2020. Nonetheless, as many as 18 works used actual datasets to train their models. Some works measured the data through experiments using their own platform, whereas other works used public datasets available across the Internet. Four papers generated synthetic datasets. They contained some parameters of the evaluated 5G environment that were randomly generated. Finally, 10 works did not describe the source of the data used to train the proposed models. This is a point of concern in our view, as it makes the reproducibility and verification of the results of these works very difficult if not impossible altogether.

Unfortunately, none of the the works that created their own datasets (through simulation, measurements, or generated synthetically) made the data available. As a result, future works cannot use them to train new deep learning models or even use their results for comparison. Indeed, the availability of datasets for cellular networks is usually restricted to researchers subject to non-disclosure agreements (NDAs) and contracts with telecommunication operators and other private companies as also confirmed by [93].

Therefore, in this section, we describe some of the few public datasets used in the works that we managed to verify during this systematic review. The idea is to provide a brief description of these datasets that may be used in new works based on deep learning and provide useful pointers to the reader on where to find these. Note that public 5G traces and datasets remain difficult to find and that most of the existing traces are relatively old and related to 4G technology.

3.4.1. Telecom Italia Big Challenge Dataset

The Telecom Italia dataset [93] was used by majority of works [6,10,41,45,46]. It was provided as apart of a *Big Data Challenge* and is composed of various open multi-source aggregations of telecommunications, weather, news, social networks and electricity data. In 2014, the data was collected from two Italian areas: the city of Milan and the Province of Trentino.

With regard to the Call Detail Records (CDRs) present in the dataset, Telecom Italia recorded the following activities: (i) data about SMS, (ii) data about incoming and outgoing calls, and (iii) data about the Internet traffic. A CDR is generated every time a user starts or terminates an Internet session, if a connection takes more than 15 min, or more than five MB is transferred during a user session.

Further, the Telecom Italia dataset also includes the Social Pulse dataset (The Social Pulse dataset is composed of geo-located tweets that were posted by users from Trentino and Milan between 1 November 2013 and 31 December 2013), and other data such as weather, electricity (only for the Tentrino region), and news. For more information about this dataset, please see [93].

It comes at no surprise that the Telecom Italia dataset was used in several papers found in this systematic review. In [45], the dataset was used to train a model for predicting the minimum, maximum, and average traffic (multitask learning) of the next hour based on the traffic of the current hour. In [6], the models were proposed to predict traffic in a city environment taking into account spatial and temporal aspects. The data was sliced using a sliding window scheme generating several samples according with the closeness and the periodicity. In [10,41], the dataset was used to train the model to detect anomalies and data for short messages (SMS), calls, and Internet usage were considered. The authors divided the dataset into samples of three-hour ranges (morning, from 6 to 9 a.m.; afternoon, from 11 to 2 p.m.; and evening, from 5 to 8 p.m.). Another work that used the dataset for traffic prediction was presented in [46]. Here the authors compiled the traffic volume from the covered areas of cells of the dataset, and then normalized to the [0, 1] range for the convenience of carrying the analysis.

3.4.2. CTU-13 Dataset

The CTU-13 dataset [94] was compiled in 2011, in CTU University, in the Czech Republic, and comprises real botnet, normal, and background traffic.

The dataset is composed of 30 captures (corresponding to different scenarios) for several botnets samples. In each scenario, a specific malware with different protocols is used. After the capture, the authors analyzed the flow data in order to create the labels. There are four types of flows in the dataset: background, botnet, command and control channels, and normal. However, the dataset is unbalanced. For example, for a given scenario, there are 114,077 flows, where 37 (0.03%) is botnet traffic, and 112,337 (98.47%) of normal traffic.

Two works found in this systematic review used this dataset [38,40] to train deep learning models for anomaly detection. The authors made two different training/testing data partition. In the first partition, the CTU dataset was divided between training (80%), and testing (20%), both containing samples of every botnet. In the second partition, the botnet flows were divided into training and testing, i.e., the botnet flows that are present in the training set were not present in testing set.

3.4.3. 4G LTE Dataset with Channel from University College Cork (UCC)

This next dataset is provided by UCC [95] and is composed of client-side cellular KPIs. The information was collected from two major Irish mobile operators for different mobility patterns (static, pedestrian, car, train, and tram). There are 135 traces in the dataset, and each trace has an average duration of 50 min and a throughput that varies from 0 to 173 Mbit/s at a granularity of one sample per second. An Android network monitoring application was used to capture several channel related KPIs, downlink and uplink throughput, context-related metrics, and also cell-related information.

In an attempt to supplement the actual measured dataset, another dataset was generated through simulation and is also provided as a 4G LTE Dataset. The popular open source public Ns-3 simulator was used to create this dataset. It includes one hundred users randomly scattered across a seven-cell cluster. The main purpose of this complementary dataset is to provide information about the base stations (not present in the real dataset). In addition, the code and context information are offered to allow other researchers to generate their own synthetic datasets.

Nonetheless, only one work found in this systematic review actually used this dataset [5]. The model proposed was trained considering as input historical network data such as donwlink bitrate, uplink bitrate, and network delay. After the training, the model is then able to predict these network performance parameters for the next 1 min time interval.

3.5. What Are the Most Common Scenarios Used to Evaluate the Integration between 5G and Deep Learning?

Evaluating the works found in this systematic review, we noted that most of the works (40 of them) considered a generic scenario in their evaluations, and that only 16 articles considered specific ones.

The urban environment tops the studies as the most common scenario presented in the works [6,34,41,44–46,48,66,67,72,75]. This is justifiable as urban scenarios are very dynamic, very challenging and heterogeneous, with the presence of different obstacles (persons, vehicles, and buildings). They reflect extreme conditions that could not be easily handled by the previous cellular generations and where 5G requires special solutions such as the use of milli-meter waves, advanced beamforming, NOMA, etc., to deliver its promises. Notably, efficient usage of the frequency spectrum and the high energy consumption are two big challenges present in these scenarios [96].

Two recent works [2,17] considered vehicular networks as use case to evaluate their solutions. These demonstrate the increased research and interest in the domain of autonomous and connected vehicles, where 5G networks play a important role, providing a low latency with high availability [97]. Vehicular networks present unprecedented challenges that are not present in traditional wireless networks, such as fast-varying wireless propagation channels and ever-changing network topology [98]. Therefore, many researchers see the use of deep learning as a promising venue to solve some the stringent 5G problems.

In [2], the authors considered two vehicular network configurations while varying the device battery capacity and the available bandwidth; and also scenarios with a smartphone transmission of high definition (720p) real-time video conferencing signals.

Three different scenarios were evaluated in [5], namely, a video medical consultation (full duplex two direction live stream uplink/downlink), a virtual treatment (propagating a single direction video live stream (downlink)) and a simple Data Submit (Single direction data exchange over the uplink).

Cellular networks can also differ in terms of device location such as when operating indoor or outdoor. Indoor environments (homes and offices) have different characteristics that outdoor ones (road intersections, squares, stadiums, etc.). Evaluations carried out in outdoor scenarios are more common in the works found in this systematic review. Additionally to the works that considered urban cities and vehicular network, the work presented in [35] considered the users location problem within the New York University campus. A hybrid setup was considered in [7]. Here two outdoor and two indoor scenarios were examined: The two outdoor scenarios were parking lots situated outside a building, while the two indoor scenarios were a workroom and an aisle inside a building.

3.6. What Are the Main Research Challenges in 5G and Deep Learning Field?

Unfortunately, the majority of the articles examined in this systematic review did not present challenges or plans for future works (29 articles). It was then difficult to identify opportunities for new researches.

From the works that present next steps for the research, we can highlight the following relevant research issues. Some works plan to evaluate their solution based on real system aspects or real datasets. Authors often cite the lack of real datasets and traces as a major drawback of their current work and resort to the use of datasets generated through simulations. Though not an error in itself, the use of synthetic data may limit the scope of the findings.

Generally, many studies point out that the complexity of the 5G scenario remains a challenge. In fact, mathematical models are more difficult to develop here which makes the use of deep learning techniques more attractive. However, although deep learning models are able to process a big variety of data and receive multi-variate input data, the solutions proposed are often simplified to achieve low computational complexity. In this line of thought, some studies plan to include and add more input parameters for their models. For example, some works plan to consider more realistic parameters about the physical medium in their systems, while others considered to add new parameters. The inclusion of these parameters can considerably increase the complexity of the scenarios to be addressed. In addition, the presence of more parameters have a direct impact on the system performance [11]. This is an issue when dealing with real-time systems as in the case of 5G. Furthermore, it is always important to determine the level of abstraction needed to study a problem. It is not always the case that more parameters and detailing of a model are guaranteed to bring more accurate results and insights. The price may be higher than the benefits.

An alternative technique can be in the use of reinforcement learning. This is known to adapt and react dynamically to the environment at hand. This paradigm does not require data for training the agent, but it needs to describe a reward function and to represent the environment so that the agent learns to take actions that optimize that reward. The problem can be that one cannot afford to let an agent take wrong decisions in an attempt to learn as these can be costly to the operation of the network. We find this kind of problem also present in other critical application domains such as medical applications were one cannot afford to the use of deep learning due to the the risk on human life it may generate.

A further challenge pointed out by [11] is to consider deep learning solutions in scenarios with massive connections. This is indeed seen as a considerable challenge due to the the presence of different mobility patterns and different wireless channel fading conditions for the thousands of users. More robust models are needed. This complex scenario can hardly be subject to the application of traditional models. Instead, deep learning models represent a powerful tool to handle the different mobility patterns (using new recurrent models obtained from historical data) and different wireless channels (for example by considering reinforcement learning for environment-based learning).

The use of deep learning can sometimes be hampered by the processing power and timeliness especially in the presence of massive numbers of devices as in the case Industry 4.0. Understandably, many papers identified as challenges and future works the need to improve the performance of their solutions. After all, the performance of the overall system is slightly dependent on that of the adopted deep learning model. To achieve such improvement, some works intend to make a fine-tuning in the solution proposed, while others plan to trim or compress their networks, and there are those who consider new deep learning models altogether, with appropriated type of layers.

Last but not least, we find it important to highlight the strong integration between IoT and 5G networks. Future IoT applications will require new performance requirements, such as massive connectivity, security, trustworthy, coverage of wireless communication, ultra-low latency, throughput, and ultra-reliable [99]. It is not a coincidence that most part of these requirements are part of the planned 5G services. The authors in [10,41] plan to evaluate their deep learning-based solutions in IoT scenarios: in [41] the authors plan to consider aspects about security (anomaly detection), while in [10] the authors plan consider energy consumption.

3.7. Discussions

As presented in this systematic review, all the selected papers are very recent as most of them were published in the year 2019 (57.1%). The oldest paper we examined is from the year 2015. This reflects the novelty and hotness of the technologies 5G and deep learning, and of course their integration.

5G is a technology in development and is set to solve several limitations present in the previous generations of cellular communication systems. It offers services, so far limited, such as massive connectivity, security, trust, large coverage, ultra-low latency (in the range of 1 ms over the air interface), throughput, and ultra-reliability, (99.999% of availability). On the other side of the spectrum, deep learning has received a lot of attention in the last few years as it has surpassed several state-of-the-art solutions in several fields, such as computer vision, text recognition, robotics, etc. The many reviewed recent publications attest the benefits that 5G technology would enjoy by making use of deep learning advances.

For the purpose of illustration only, as commented in [11], resource allocation in real cellular wireless networks can be formulated and solved using tools from optimization theory. However, the solutions often used have a high computational complexity. deep learning models may be a surrogate solution keeping the same performance but with reduced computational complexity.

We also noted that many works (a total of 25 to be precise) were published in conferences with few pages (around six pages). We believe that they represent works in progress, as they only show initial results. It reinforces the general view that the the integration between 5G and deep learning is still an evolving area of interest with many advances and contributions expected soon.

By observing the different scenarios considered in the examined articles, they generally do not focus on a real application (30 out of 57 articles found). However, a project called Mobile and wireless communications Enablers for the Twenty-twenty Information Society (METIS) published a document that explained several 5G scenarios and their specific requirements [100]. Nine use cases are presented: gaming, marathon, media on demand, unnamed aerial vehicles, remote tactile interaction, e-health, ultra-low cost 5G network, remote car sensing and control, and forest industry on remote control. Each of these scenarios have different characteristics and different requirements regarding 5G networks. For instance, remote tactile iterations scenarios can be considered a critical application (e.g., remote surgeries) and demand ultra-low latency (not be greater than 2 ms) and high reliability (99.999%). On the other hand, in the marathon use case, the participants commonly use attached tracing devices. This scenario must handle thousands of users simultaneously requiring high signaling efficiency and user capacity. As result, we believe that in order to achieve high impact results, deep learning solutions need to be targeted towards addressing use cases with specific requirements instead of trying to deal with the more general picture. Planning deep learning models for dynamic scenarios can be a complex task, since deep learning models need to capture the patterns present in the dataset. Thus, if the data varies widely between scenarios, it can certainly impact the performance of the models. One approach that can be used to deal with this limitation is the use of reinforcement learning. As presented in Section 3.2, seven works considered this paradigm in their solutions. Indeed, this approach considers training software agents to react to the environment in order to maximize (or minimize) a metric of interest. This paradigm can be a good approach to train software agents to dynamically adapt according to changes in the environment, and thus meet the different requirements of the use cases presented above.

However, reinforcement learning requires an environment where the software agent needs to be inserted during their training. Simulators can be a good approach, due the low cost of implementation. For example, consider an agent trained to control physical medium parameters instead of having to manually set up these, e.g., by fine tuning rules and thresholds. After training, the agent must be placed in a scenario with greater fidelity for validation, for example a prototype that can represent a real scenario. Finally, the reinforcement learning agent can be deployed in a software-driven solution in the real scenario. These steps are necessary to avoid the drawbacks to deploying a non trained agent within a real operating 5G network. This is a cost, operators cannot afford.

4. Final Considerations

This work presented a systematic review on the use of deep learning models to solve 5G-related problems. 5G stands to benefit from deep learning as reported in this review. Though these models remove some of the traditional modeling complexity, developers need to determine the right balance between performance and abstraction level. More detailed models are not necessarily more powerful and many times the added complexity cannot be justified.

The review has also shown that the used deep learning techniques range across a plethora of possibilities. A developer must carefully opt for the right strategy to a given problem. We also showed that many works developed hybrid approaches in an attempt to cover a whole problem. Deep learning techniques are often also combined in the case of 5G with optimization algorithms such as genetic algorithm among others to produce optimized solutions.

Establishing clear use cases is important to determine the scope of a problem and therefore the deep learning parameters applied to it. 5G is known to offer services that have different and sometimes conflicting requirements. Hence, a solution that works for a given scenario may not work for another one.

Deep learning techniques are known to be data based. The more data, the most testing and development can be done and consequently, the better models we can produce. Unfortunately, due to reasons of business privacy very limited datasets are available. This is in contrast to other research communities that offer several datasets for research as in the case of image processing for example. We therefore believe that the industry and scientific community must make a similar effort to create more recent and representative 5G datasets. The use of simulated, old, and synthetic data has major limitations and may have questionable results.

A major point of concern in the 5G and deep learning integration remains that of performance. As we are dealing with real-time problems, the adopted solutions must not only deliver the expected solution but they must do it at the right time. Two things emerge from this point. The first one is related to the scope of deep-learning applications. In this case, we need to be careful in using it for problems that require agile answers sometimes at the nanosecond level. A second approach would be to develop simpler or compressed models.

Overall, the use of deep learning in 5G has already produced many important contributions and one expects these to evolve even further in the near future despite the many limitations identified in this review.

Author Contributions: Conceptualization, G.L.S. and P.T.E.; methodology, G.L.S. and P.T.E.; validation, G.L.S. and P.T.E.; formal analysis, G.L.S. and P.T.E.; investigation, G.L.S. and P.T.E.; resources, G.L.S. and P.T.E.; writing-original draft preparation, G.L.S. and P.T.E.; writing-review and editing, G.L.S., P.T.E., J.K., and D.S.; visualization, G.L.S. and P.T.E.; supervision, J.K. and D.J. All authors have read and agreed to the published version of the manuscript.

Acknowledgments: The authors would like to thank the Fundação de Amparo a Ciência e Tecnologia de Pernambuco (FACEPE) for funding this work through grant IBPG-0059-1.03/19.

Conflicts of Interest: The authors declare no conflict of interest.

Appendix A

The Table A1 presents a summary of all works covered in this systematic review. Each row is about a paper and describes briefly the type of DL used in the paper, the learning type, the data source, and the paper objective using DL.

Table A1. Summary of works found in this systematic review.

Article	Layer Type	Learning Type	Data Source	Paper Objective
[56]	fully connected	supervised	simulation	to use a deep learning approach to reduce the network energy consumption and the transmission delay via optimizing the placement of content in heterogeneous networks.
[61]	DBN	supervised	simulation	a deep learning model was used to find the approximated optimal joint resource allocation strategy to minimize the energy consumption
[76]	fully connected	supervised	synthetic	the paper proposed a deep learning model to multiuser detection problem in the scenario of SCMA
[25]	autoencoder	unsupervised	simulation	the paper proposed the use of autoencoders to reduce PAPR in OFDM techniques called PRNet. The model is used to map constellation mapping and demapping of symbols on each subcarrier in an OFDM system, while minimize BER
[19]	residual network	supervised	synthetic	a deep-learning model was proposed for CSI estimation in FBMC systems. The traditional CSI estimation and equalization and demapping module are replaced by deep learning model
[67]	not described	supervised	real data	the paper propose a solution for optimize the self-organization in LTE networks. The solution, called APP-SON, makes the optimization based on the applications characteristics
[70]	a memory with custom memory	supervised and unsupervised	not described	the work proposed a digital cancellation scheme eliminating linear and non-linear interference based on deep learning
[38]	DBN	supervised	real data	the paper proposed a deep learning-based solution for anomaly detection on 5G network flows
[26]	fully connected and LSTM	supervised	not described	the authors proposed a deep learning model for channel decoding. The model is based on polar and LDPC mechanisms for decode signals in the receiver devices
[59]	LSTM	supervised	simulation	the authors proposed a machine learning-based solution to predict the medium usage for network slices in 5G environments meeting some SLA requirements
[34]	CNN	supervised	simulation	the authors proposed a system to to convert the received millimeter wave radiation into the device's position using CNN

Table A1. Cont.

Article	Layer Type	Learning Type	Data Source	Paper Objective
[71]	biLSTM	supervised	real data	a BiLSTM model was used to represent the effects of non-linear PAs, which is a promising technology for 5G. The authors defined the map between the digital baseband stimuluses and the response as a non-linear function.
[6]	CNN	supervised	real data	the authors proposed a framework based on CNN models to predict traffic in a city environment taking into account spatial and temporal aspects
[21]	fully connected	supervised	not described	the authors proposed a deep learning scheme to represent a constellation-domain multiplexing at the transmitter. This scheme was used to parameterize the bit-to-symbol mapping as well as the symbol detector
[23]	autoencoder	supervised	not described	the paper proposes a deep learning model to learning automatically the codebook SCMA. The codebook is responsible to code the transmitted bits into multidimensional codewords. Thus, the model proposed maps the bits into a resource (codebook) after the transmission and decode the signal received into bits at the receiver
[51]	LSTM	supervised	simulation	the paper proposed deep learning based scheme to avoid handover failures based on early prediction. This scheme can be used to evaluate the signal condition and make the handover before a failure happen
[7]	CNN and LSTM	supervised	real data	the authors proposed an online framework to estimate CSI based on deep learning models called OCEAN. OCEAN is able to find CSI for a mobile device during a period ate a specific place
[3]	not described	deep learning and reinforcement learning	not described	the authors proposed a beamforming scheme based on deep reinforcement learning. The problem addressed was the beamforming performance in dynamic environments. Depends on the number of users concentrated in a area, the beamforming configuration is produce a more directed signal, on the other hand a signal with wide coverage is sent. The solution proposed is composed of three different models. The first one, is a model that generated synthetic user mobility patterns. The second model tries to response with a more appropriated antenna diagram (beamforming configuration). The third model evaluates the performance of results obtained by the models and returns a reward for the previous models. The authors did not make any experiments about the scheme proposed

Table A1. Cont.

Article	Layer Type	Learning Type	Data Source	Paper Objective
[15]	fully connected	supervised	simulation	the authors proposed a deep learning scheme for DD-CE in MIMO systems. The core part of DD-CE is the channel prediction, where the "current channel state is estimated base on the previous estimate and detected symbols". Deep learning can avoid the need of complex mathematical models for doppler rates estimation
[16]	fully connected	supervised	simulation	the authors combined deep learning and superimposed coding techniques for CSI feedback. In a traditional superimposed coding-based CSI feedback system, the main goal of a base station is to recover downlink CSI and detect user data
[63]	fully connected	supervised	simulation	the authors proposed an algorithm to allocate carrier in MCPA dynamically, taking into account the energy efficiency and the implementation complexity. The main idea is to minimize the total power consumption finding the optimal carrier to MPCA allocation. To solve this problem, two approaches were used: convex relaxation and deep learning
[29]	CNN	supervised	not described	the authors presented a deep learning model to fault detection and fault location in wireless communication systems through deep learning, focusing in mmWave systems
[44]	3D CNN	supervised	real data	the authors proposed a deep learning-based solution for allocation resources previously based on data analytic. The solution is called DeepCog, which receives as input measurement data of a specific network slice, make a prediction of network flow and allocate resources in data center to meet the demand
[17]	fully connected and RNN	supervised	simulation	the authors proposed a systematic review about CSI and then presented some evaluations using deep learning models. The solutions presented in the systematic review have a focus on "linear correlations such as sparse spatial steering vectors or frequency response, and Gauss-Markov time correlations"
[36]	LSTM	supervised	simulation	the authors proposed a deep learning-based algorithm for handover mechanism. The model is used to predict the user mobility and anticipate the handover preparation previously. The algorithm will estimate the future position of the an user based on its historical data

Table A1. Cont.

Article	Layer Type	Learning Type	Data Source	Paper Objective
[62]	fully connected	deep learning and reinforcement learning	simulation	the authors proposed a solution to improve the energy efficiency of user equipment in MEC environments in 5G. In the work, two different types of applications were considered: URLLC and high data rate delay tolerant applications. The solution uses a "digital twin" of the real network to train the neural network models
[11]	fully connected	supervised	synthetic (through genetic algorithm)	the authors proposed a deep learning model for resource allocation to maximize the network throughput by performing joint resource allocation (i.e., both power and channel). Firstly a review about deep learning techniques applied to wireless resource allocations problem was presented. After, a deep learning model was presented. This model takes as input the CQI and the location indicator (position between the user from the base stations) of users for all base stations and predicts the power and sub-band allocations
[68]	fully connected	supervised	simulation	the work proposed a pilot allocation scheme based on deep learning for massive MIMO systems. The model was used to learn the relationship between the users' location and the near-optimal pilot assignment with low computational complexity
[65]	fully connected	supervised	not described	the authors proposed a deep learning model for smart communication systems for highly density D2D mmWave environments using beamforming. The model can be used to predict the best relay for relaying data taking into account several reliability metrics for select the relay node (e.g., another device or a base station)
[64]	fully connected	supervised	simulation	the authors proposed a deep learning-based solution for downlink CoMP in 5G environments. The model receives as input some physical layer measurements from the connected user equipment and "formulates a modified CoMP trigger function to enhance the downlink capacity". The output of the model is the decision to enable/disable the CoMP mechanism
[22]	fully connected	supervised	not described	the authors proposed a deep learning-based scheme for precoding and SIC decoding for scheme for the MIMO-NOMA system

Table A1. Cont.

Article	Layer Type	Learning Type	Data Source	Paper Objective
[57]	LSTM	supervised and reinforcement learning	simulation	the authors proposed a framework to resource scheduling allocation based on deep learning and reinforcement learning. The main goal is to minimize the resource consumption at the same time guaranteeing the required performance isolation degree. A LSTM and reinforcement learning are used in cooperation to do this task. A LSTM model was used to predict the traffic based on the historical data.
[45]	LSTM, 3D CNN, and CNN+LSTM	supervised	real data	the authors proposed a multitask learning based on deep learning for predict data flow in 5G environments. The model is able to predict the minimum, maximum, and average traffic (multitask learn) of the next hour based on the traffic of the current hour.
[30]	DBN	unsupervised and supervised	real data	the authors proposed a DBN model for fault location in optical fronthaul networks. The model proposed identify faults and false alarms in alarm information considering single link connections
[41]	fully connected	supervised	real data	the paper proposed a deep learning model to detect anomalies in the network traffic, considering two types of behavior as network anomalies: sleeping cells and soared traffic.
[47]	LSTM	supervised	simulation	the authors proposed a deep learning model to predict traffic in base stations in order to avoid flow congestion in 5G ultra dense networks
[52]	fully connected and LSTM	supervised	real data	the authors proposed a analytical model for holistic handover cost and a deep learning model to handover prediction. The holistic handover cost model takes into account signaling overhead, latency, call dropping, and radio resource wastage
[48]	LSTM	supervised	real data	a system model that combine mobile edge computing and mobile data offloading was proposed in the paper. In order to improve the system performance, a deep learning model was proposed to predict the traffic and decide if the offloading can be performed on the base station
[55]	-	reinforcement learning	simulation	the authors proposed a network architecture that integrates MEC and C-RAN. In order to reduce the latency, a caching mechanism can be adopted in the MEC. Thus, reinforcement learning was used to maximize the cache hit rate the cache use

Table A1. Cont.

Article	Layer Type	Learning Type	Data Source	Paper Objective
[46]	LSTM	supervised	real data	the paper proposed a framework to cluster RRHs and map them into BBU pools using predicted data of mobile traffic. Firstly, the future traffic of the RRHs are estimated using a deep learning model based on the historical traffic data, then these RRHs are grouped according with their complementarity
[40]	DBN	supervised	real data	the paper proposes a deep learning-based approach to analyze network flows and detect network anomalies. This approach executes in a MEC in 5G networks. A system based on NFV and SDN was proposed to detect and react to anomalies in the network
[77]	-	reinforcement learning	simulation	the paper proposed two schemes based on Q-learning to choose the best downlink and uplink configuration in dynamic TDD systems. The main goal is to optimize the MOS, which is a QoE measure that correspond a better experience of users.
[35]	CNN, LSTM, and temporal convolutional network	supervised	simulation	the authors proposed a deep learning-based approach to predict the user position for mmwave systems based on beamformed fingerprint
[2]	LSTM	supervised and reinforcement learning	simulation	the authors deal with physical layer control problem. A reinforcement learning-based solution was used to learn the optimal physical-layer control parameters of different scenarios. The scheme proposed use reinforcement learning to choose the best configuration for the scenario. In the scheme proposed, a radio designer need to specify the network configuration that varies according with the scenario specification
[58]	X-LSTM	supervised	real data	the paper proposed models to predict the mount of PRBs available to allocate network slices in 5G networks
[66]	fully connected	supervised	real data	the authors proposed a algorithm to achieve self-optimization in LTE and 5G networks trough wireless analysis. The deep learning model is used to perform a regression to derive the relationship between the engineering parameters and the performance indicators
[10]	fully connected	supervised	real data	the paper proposed a deep learning-based solution to detect anomalies in 5G networks powered by MEC. The model detects sleeping cells events and soared traffic as anomalies
[60]	fully connected	supervised	simulation	the paper proposed a framework to optimize the energy consumption of NOMA systems in a resource allocation problem.

Table A1. *Cont.*

Article	Layer Type	Learning Type	Data Source	Paper Objective
[72]	fully connected	supervised	simulation	the paper proposed an auction mechanism for spectrum sharing using deep learning models in order to improve the channel capacity
[73]	fully connected	supervised and reinforcement learning	simulation	the paper proposed a deep reinforcement learning mechanism for packet scheduler in multi-path networks.
[5]	Generative adversarial networks (GAN) with LSTM and CNN layers	supervised	real data	the paper proposed a deep learning-based framework for address the problem of the network slicing scheme for the mobile network. The deep learning model is used to predict network flow in other to make resource allocation
[27]	Autoencoder with Bi-GRU layers	supervised	not described	the paper proposed a deep learning-based solution for channel coding in low-latency scenarios. The idea was to create a robust and adaptable mechanism for generic codes for future communications
[74]	fully connected	supervised	synthetic	the paper proposed a deep learning model for physical layer security. The model was used to optimize the value of the power allocation factor in a secure communication system
[75]	CNN and fully connected	supervised	simulation	the paper proposed a radio propagation model based on deep learning. The model maps geographical area in the radio propagation (path loss)
[24]	partially and fully connected layers	unsupervised	not described	a deep learning model was proposed to represent a MU-SIMO system. The main purpose is to reduce the difference between the signal transmitted and the signal received
[43]	GRU	supervised	real data	the paper proposed a deep learning-based framework for traffic prediction in order to enable proactive adjustment in network slice

References

1. Cisco. Global—2021 Forecast Highlights. 2016. Available online: https://www.cisco.com/c/dam/m/en_us/solutions/service-provider/vni-forecast-highlights/pdf/Global_2021_Forecast_Highlights.pdf (accessed on 19 August 2020).
2. Joseph, S.; Misra, R.; Katti, S. Towards self-driving radios: Physical-layer control using deep reinforcement learning. In Proceedings of the 20th International Workshop on Mobile Computing Systems and Applications, Santa Cruz, CA, USA, 27–28 February 2019; pp. 69–74.
3. Maksymyuk, T.; Gazda, J.; Yaremko, O.; Nevinskiy, D. Deep Learning Based Massive MIMO Beamforming for 5G Mobile Network. In Proceedings of the 2018 IEEE 4th International Symposium on Wireless Systems within the International Conferences on Intelligent Data Acquisition and Advanced Computing Systems (IDAACS-SWS), Lviv, Ukraine, 20–21 September 2018; pp. 241–244.

4. Arteaga, C.H.T.; Anacona, F.B.; Ortega, K.T.T.; Rendon, O.M.C. A Scaling Mechanism for an Evolved Packet Core based on Network Functions Virtualization. *IEEE Trans. Netw. Serv. Manag.* **2019**, *17*, 779–792. [CrossRef]
5. Gu, R.; Zhang, J. GANSlicing: A GAN-Based Software Defined Mobile Network Slicing Scheme for IoT Applications. In Proceedings of the 2019 IEEE International Conference on Communications (ICC), Shanghai, China, 20–24 May 2019; pp. 1–7.
6. Zhang, C.; Zhang, H.; Yuan, D.; Zhang, M. Citywide cellular traffic prediction based on densely connected convolutional neural networks. *IEEE Commun. Lett.* **2018**, *22*, 1656–1659. [CrossRef]
7. Luo, C.; Ji, J.; Wang, Q.; Chen, X.; Li, P. Channel state information prediction for 5G wireless communications: A deep learning approach. *IEEE Trans. Netw. Sci. Eng.* **2018**, *7*, 227–236. [CrossRef]
8. Goodfellow, I.; Bengio, Y.; Courville, A.; Bengio, Y. *Deep Learning*; MIT Press: Cambridge, UK, 2016; Volume 1.
9. LeCun, Y.; Bengio, Y.; Hinton, G. Deep learning. *Nature* **2015**, *521*, 436. [CrossRef]
10. Hussain, B.; Du, Q.; Zhang, S.; Imran, A.; Imran, M.A. Mobile Edge Computing-Based Data-Driven Deep Learning Framework for Anomaly Detection. *IEEE Access* **2019**, *7*, 137656–137667. [CrossRef]
11. Ahmed, K.I.; Tabassum, H.; Hossain, E. Deep learning for radio resource allocation in multi-cell networks. *IEEE Netw.* **2019**, *33*, 188–195. [CrossRef]
12. Zhang, C.; Patras, P.; Haddadi, H. Deep learning in mobile and wireless networking: A survey. *IEEE Commun. Surv. Tutor.* **2019**, *21*, 2224–2287. [CrossRef]
13. Coutinho, E.F.; de Carvalho Sousa, F.R.; Rego, P.A.L.; Gomes, D.G.; de Souza, J.N. Elasticity in cloud computing: A survey. *Ann. Telecommun.* **2015**, *70*, 289–309. [CrossRef]
14. Caire, G.; Jindal, N.; Kobayashi, M.; Ravindran, N. Multiuser MIMO achievable rates with downlink training and channel state feedback. *IEEE Trans. Inf. Theory* **2010**, *56*, 2845–2866. [CrossRef]
15. Mehrabi, M.; Mohammadkarimi, M.; Ardakani, M.; Jing, Y. Decision Directed Channel Estimation Based on Deep Neural Network k-Step Predictor for MIMO Communications in 5G. *IEEE J. Sel. Areas Commun.* **2019**, *37*, 2443–2456. [CrossRef]
16. Qing, C.; Cai, B.; Yang, Q.; Wang, J.; Huang, C. Deep learning for CSI feedback based on superimposed coding. *IEEE Access* **2019**, *7*, 93723–93733. [CrossRef]
17. Jiang, Z.; Chen, S.; Molisch, A.F.; Vannithamby, R.; Zhou, S.; Niu, Z. Exploiting wireless channel state information structures beyond linear correlations: A deep learning approach. *IEEE Commun. Mag.* **2019**, *57*, 28–34. [CrossRef]
18. Prasad, K.S.V.; Hossain, E.; Bhargava, V.K. Energy efficiency in massive MIMO-based 5G networks: Opportunities and challenges. *IEEE Wirel. Commun.* **2017**, *24*, 86–94. [CrossRef]
19. Cheng, X.; Liu, D.; Zhu, Z.; Shi, W.; Li, Y. A ResNet-DNN based channel estimation and equalization scheme in FBMC/OQAM systems. In Proceedings of the 2018 10th International Conference on Wireless Communications and Signal Processing (WCSP), Hangzhou, China, 18–20 October 2018; pp. 1–5.
20. Ez-Zazi, I.; Arioua, M.; El Oualkadi, A.; Lorenz, P. A hybrid adaptive coding and decoding scheme for multi-hop wireless sensor networks. *Wirel. Pers. Commun.* **2017**, *94*, 3017–3033. [CrossRef]
21. Jiang, L.; Li, X.; Ye, N.; Wang, A. Deep Learning-Aided Constellation Design for Downlink NOMA. In Proceedings of the 2019 15th International Wireless Communications & Mobile Computing Conference (IWCMC), Tangier, Morocco, 24–28 June 2019; pp. 1879–1883.
22. Kang, J.M.; Kim, I.M.; Chun, C.J. Deep Learning-Based MIMO-NOMA With Imperfect SIC Decoding. *IEEE Syst. J.* **2019**. [CrossRef]
23. Kim, M.; Kim, N.I.; Lee, W.; Cho, D.H. Deep learning-aided SCMA. *IEEE Commun. Lett.* **2018**, *22*, 720–723. [CrossRef]
24. Xue, S.; Ma, Y.; Yi, N.; Tafazolli, R. Unsupervised deep learning for MU-SIMO joint transmitter and noncoherent receiver design. *IEEE Wirel. Commun. Lett.* **2018**, *8*, 177–180. [CrossRef]
25. Kim, M.; Lee, W.; Cho, D.H. A novel PAPR reduction scheme for OFDM system based on deep learning. *IEEE Commun. Lett.* **2017**, *22*, 510–513. [CrossRef]
26. Wang, Y.; Zhang, Z.; Zhang, S.; Cao, S.; Xu, S. A unified deep learning based polar-LDPC decoder for 5G communication systems. In Proceedings of the 2018 10th International Conference on Wireless Communications and Signal Processing (WCSP), Hangzhou, China, 18–20 October 2018; pp. 1–6.

27. Jiang, Y.; Kim, H.; Asnani, H.; Kannan, S.; Oh, S.; Viswanath, P. Learn codes: Inventing low-latency codes via recurrent neural networks. In Proceedings of the 2019 IEEE International Conference on Communications (ICC), Shanghai, China, 20–24 May 2019; pp. 1–7.
28. Hu, P.; Zhang, J. 5G Enabled Fault Detection and Diagnostics: How Do We Achieve Efficiency? *IEEE Internet Things J.* **2020**, *7*, 3267–3281. [CrossRef]
29. Chen, K.; Wang, W.; Chen, X.; Yin, H. Deep Learning Based Antenna Array Fault Detection. In Proceedings of the 2019 IEEE 89th Vehicular Technology Conference (VTC2019), Honolulu, HI, USA, 22–25 September 2019; pp. 1–5.
30. Yu, A.; Yang, H.; Yao, Q.; Li, Y.; Guo, H.; Peng, T.; Li, H.; Zhang, J. Accurate Fault Location Using Deep Belief Network for Optical Fronthaul Networks in 5G and Beyond. *IEEE Access* **2019**, *7*, 77932–77943. [CrossRef]
31. Xiong, H.; Zhang, D.; Zhang, D.; Gauthier, V.; Yang, K.; Becker, M. MPaaS: Mobility prediction as a service in telecom cloud. *Inf. Syst. Front.* **2014**, *16*, 59–75. [CrossRef]
32. Cheng, Y.; Qiao, Y.; Yang, J. An improved Markov method for prediction of user mobility. In Proceedings of the 2016 12th International Conference on Network and Service Management (CNSM), Montreal, QC, Canada, 31 October–4 November 2016; pp. 394–399.
33. Qiao, Y.; Yang, J.; He, H.; Cheng, Y.; Ma, Z. User location prediction with energy efficiency model in the Long Term-Evolution network. *Int. J. Commun. Syst.* **2016**, *29*, 2169–2187. [CrossRef]
34. Gante, J.; Falcão, G.; Sousa, L. Beamformed fingerprint learning for accurate millimeter wave positioning. In Proceedings of the 2018 IEEE 88th Vehicular Technology Conference (VTC-Fall), Chicago, IL, USA, 27–30 August 2018; pp. 1–5.
35. Gante, J.; Falcão, G.; Sousa, L. Deep Learning Architectures for Accurate Millimeter Wave Positioning in 5G. *Neural Process. Lett.* **2019**. [CrossRef]
36. Wang, C.; Zhao, Z.; Sun, Q.; Zhang, H. Deep learning-based intelligent dual connectivity for mobility management in dense network. In Proceedings of the 2018 IEEE 88th Vehicular Technology Conference (VTC-Fall), Chicago, IL, USA, 27–30 August 2018; pp. 1–5.
37. Santos, J.; Leroux, P.; Wauters, T.; Volckaert, B.; De Turck, F. Anomaly detection for smart city applications over 5g low power wide area networks. In Proceedings of the 2018 IEEE/IFIP Network Operations and Management Symposium, Taipei, Taiwan, 23–27 April 2018; pp. 1–9.
38. Maimó, L.F.; Gómez, Á.L.P.; Clemente, F.J.G.; Pérez, M.G.; Pérez, G.M. A self-adaptive deep learning-based system for anomaly detection in 5G networks. *IEEE Access* **2018**, *6*, 7700–7712. [CrossRef]
39. Parwez, M.S.; Rawat, D.B.; Garuba, M. Big data analytics for user-activity analysis and user-anomaly detection in mobile wireless network. *IEEE Trans. Ind. Inform.* **2017**, *13*, 2058–2065. [CrossRef]
40. Maimó, L.F.; Celdrán, A.H.; Pérez, M.G.; Clemente, F.J.G.; Pérez, G.M. Dynamic management of a deep learning-based anomaly detection system for 5G networks. *J. Ambient Intell. Humaniz. Comput.* **2019**, *10*, 3083–3097. [CrossRef]
41. Hussain, B.; Du, Q.; Ren, P. Deep learning-based big data-assisted anomaly detection in cellular networks. In Proceedings of the 2018 IEEE Global Communications Conference (GLOBECOM), Abu Dhabi, UAE, 9–13 December 2018; pp. 1–6.
42. Li, R.; Zhao, Z.; Zheng, J.; Mei, C.; Cai, Y.; Zhang, H. The learning and prediction of application-level traffic data in cellular networks. *IEEE Trans. Wirel. Commun.* **2017**, *16*, 3899–3912. [CrossRef]
43. Guo, Q.; Gu, R.; Wang, Z.; Zhao, T.; Ji, Y.; Kong, J.; Gour, R.; Jue, J.P. Proactive Dynamic Network Slicing with Deep Learning Based Short-Term Traffic Prediction for 5G Transport Network. In Proceedings of the 2019 Optical Fiber Communications Conference and Exhibition (OFC), San Diego, CA, USA, 3–7 March 2019; pp. 1–3.
44. Bega, D.; Gramaglia, M.; Fiore, M.; Banchs, A.; Costa-Perez, X. DeepCog: Cognitive network management in sliced 5G networks with deep learning. In Proceedings of the IEEE INFOCOM 2019—IEEE Conference on Computer Communications, Paris, France, 29 April–2 May 2019; pp. 280–288.
45. Huang, C.W.; Chiang, C.T.; Li, Q. A study of deep learning networks on mobile traffic forecasting. In Proceedings of the 2017 IEEE 28th Annual International Symposium on Personal, Indoor, and Mobile Radio Communications (PIMRC), Montreal, QC, Canada, 8–13 October 2017; pp. 1–6.
46. Chen, L.; Yang, D.; Zhang, D.; Wang, C.; Li, J. Deep mobile traffic forecast and complementary base station clustering for C-RAN optimization. *J. Netw. Comput. Appl.* **2018**, *121*, 59–69. [CrossRef]

47. Zhou, Y.; Fadlullah, Z.M.; Mao, B.; Kato, N. A deep-learning-based radio resource assignment technique for 5G ultra dense networks. *IEEE Netw.* **2018**, *32*, 28–34. [CrossRef]
48. Zhao, X.; Yang, K.; Chen, Q.; Peng, D.; Jiang, H.; Xu, X.; Shuang, X. Deep learning based mobile data offloading in mobile edge computing systems. *Future Gener. Comput. Syst.* **2019**, *99*, 346–355. [CrossRef]
49. Hosny, K.M.; Khashaba, M.M.; Khedr, W.I.; Amer, F.A. New vertical handover prediction schemes for LTE-WLAN heterogeneous networks. *PLoS ONE* **2019**, *14*, e0215334. [CrossRef] [PubMed]
50. Svahn, C.; Sysoev, O.; Cirkic, M.; Gunnarsson, F.; Berglund, J. Inter-frequency radio signal quality prediction for handover, evaluated in 3GPP LTE. In Proceedings of the 2019 IEEE 89th Vehicular Technology Conference (VTC2019), Kuala Lumpur, Malaysia, 28 April–1 May 2019; pp. 1–5.
51. Khunteta, S.; Chavva, A.K.R. Deep learning based link failure mitigation. In Proceedings of the 2017 16th IEEE International Conference on Machine Learning and Applications (ICMLA), Cancun, Mexico, 18–21 December 2017; pp. 806–811.
52. Ozturk, M.; Gogate, M.; Onireti, O.; Adeel, A.; Hussain, A.; Imran, M.A. A novel deep learning driven, low-cost mobility prediction approach for 5G cellular networks: The case of the Control/Data Separation Architecture (CDSA). *Neurocomputing* **2019**, *358*, 479–489. [CrossRef]
53. Wen, J.; Huang, K.; Yang, S.; Li, V.O. Cache-enabled heterogeneous cellular networks: Optimal tier-level content placement. *IEEE Trans. Wirel. Commun.* **2017**, *16*, 5939–5952. [CrossRef]
54. Serbetci, B.; Goseling, J. Optimal geographical caching in heterogeneous cellular networks with nonhomogeneous helpers. *arXiv* **2017**, arXiv: 1710.09626.
55. Chien, W.C.; Weng, H.Y.; Lai, C.F. Q-learning based collaborative cache allocation in mobile edge computing. *Future Gener. Comput. Syst.* **2020**, *102*, 603–610. [CrossRef]
56. Lei, L.; You, L.; Dai, G.; Vu, T.X.; Yuan, D.; Chatzinotas, S. A deep learning approach for optimizing content delivering in cache-enabled HetNet. In Proceedings of the 2017 International Symposium on Wireless Communication Systems (ISWCS), Bologna, Italy, 28–31 August 2017; pp. 449–453.
57. Yan, M.; Feng, G.; Zhou, J.; Sun, Y.; Liang, Y.C. Intelligent resource scheduling for 5G radio access network slicing. *IEEE Trans. Veh. Technol.* **2019**, *68*, 7691–7703. [CrossRef]
58. Gutterman, C.; Grinshpun, E.; Sharma, S.; Zussman, G. RAN resource usage prediction for a 5G slice broker. In Proceedings of the 20th ACM International Symposium on Mobile Ad Hoc Networking and Computing, Catania, Italy, 2–5 July 2019; pp. 231–240.
59. Toscano, M.; Grunwald, F.; Richart, M.; Baliosian, J.; Grampín, E.; Castro, A. Machine Learning Aided Network Slicing. In Proceedings of the 2019 21st International Conference on Transparent Optical Networks (ICTON), Angerrs, France, 9–13 July 2019; pp. 1–4.
60. Lei, L.; You, L.; He, Q.; Vu, T.X.; Chatzinotas, S.; Yuan, D.; Ottersten, B. Learning-assisted optimization for energy-efficient scheduling in deadline-aware NOMA systems. *IEEE Trans. Green Commun. Netw.* **2019**, *3*, 615–627. [CrossRef]
61. Luo, J.; Tang, J.; So, D.K.; Chen, G.; Cumanan, K.; Chambers, J.A. A deep learning-based approach to power minimization in multi-carrier NOMA with SWIPT. *IEEE Access* **2019**, *7*, 17450–17460. [CrossRef]
62. Dong, R.; She, C.; Hardjawana, W.; Li, Y.; Vucetic, B. Deep learning for hybrid 5G services in mobile edge computing systems: Learn from a digital twin. *IEEE Trans. Wirel. Commun.* **2019**, *18*, 4692–4707. [CrossRef]
63. Zhang, S.; Xiang, C.; Cao, S.; Xu, S.; Zhu, J. Dynamic Carrier to MCPA Allocation for Energy Efficient Communication: Convex Relaxation Versus Deep Learning. *IEEE Trans. Green Commun. Netw.* **2019**, *3*, 628–640. [CrossRef]
64. Mismar, F.B.; Evans, B.L. Deep Learning in Downlink Coordinated Multipoint in New Radio Heterogeneous Networks. *IEEE Wirel. Commun. Lett.* **2019**, *8*, 1040–1043. [CrossRef]
65. Abdelreheem, A.; Omer, O.A.; Esmaiel, H.; Mohamed, U.S. Deep learning-based relay selection in D2D millimeter wave communications. In Proceedings of the 2019 International Conference on Computer and Information Sciences (ICCIS), Aljouf, Saudi Arabia, 10–11 April 2019; pp. 1–5.
66. Ouyang, Y.; Li, Z.; Su, L.; Lu, W.; Lin, Z. APP-SON: Application characteristics-driven SON to optimize 4G/5G network performance and quality of experience. In Proceedings of the 2017 IEEE International Conference on Big Data (Big Data), Boston, MA, USA, 11–14 December 2017; pp. 1514–1523.
67. Ouyang, Y.; Li, Z.; Su, L.; Lu, W.; Lin, Z. Application behaviors Driven Self-Organizing Network (SON) for 4G LTE networks. *IEEE Trans. Netw. Sci. Eng.* **2018**, *7*, 3–14. [CrossRef]

68. Kim, K.; Lee, J.; Choi, J. Deep learning based pilot allocation scheme (DL-PAS) for 5G massive MIMO system. *IEEE Commun. Lett.* **2018**, *22*, 828–831. [CrossRef]
69. Jose, J.; Ashikhmin, A.; Marzetta, T.L.; Vishwanath, S. Pilot contamination problem in multi-cell TDD systems. In Proceedings of the 2009 IEEE International Symposium on Information Theory, Seoul, Korea, 21–26 June 2009; pp. 2184–2188.
70. Zhang, W.; Yin, J.; Wu, D.; Guo, G.; Lai, Z. A Self-Interference Cancellation Method Based on Deep Learning for Beyond 5G Full-Duplex System. In Proceedings of the 2018 IEEE International Conference on Signal Processing, Communications and Computing (ICSPCC), Qingdao, China, 14–17 September 2018; pp. 1–5.
71. Sun, J.; Shi, W.; Yang, Z.; Yang, J.; Gui, G. Behavioral modeling and linearization of wideband RF power amplifiers using BiLSTM networks for 5G wireless systems. *IEEE Trans. Veh. Technol.* **2019**, *68*, 10348–10356. [CrossRef]
72. Zhao, F.; Zhang, Y.; Wang, Q. Multi-slot spectrum auction in heterogeneous networks based on deep feedforward network. *IEEE Access* **2018**, *6*, 45113–45119. [CrossRef]
73. Roselló, M.M. Multi-path Scheduling with Deep Reinforcement Learning. In Proceedings of the 2019 European Conference on Networks and Communications (EuCNC), Valencia, Spain, 18–21 June 2019; pp. 400–405.
74. Jameel, F.; Khan, W.U.; Chang, Z.; Ristaniemi, T.; Liu, J. Secrecy analysis and learning-based optimization of cooperative NOMA SWIPT systems. In Proceedings of the 2019 IEEE International Conference on Communications Workshops (ICC Workshops), Shanghai, China, 20–24 May 2019; pp. 1–6.
75. Imai, T.; Kitao, K.; Inomata, M. Radio propagation prediction model using convolutional neural networks by deep learning. In Proceedings of the 2019 13th European Conference on Antennas and Propagation (EuCAP), Krakow, Poland, 31 March–5 April 2019; pp. 1–5.
76. Lu, C.; Xu, W.; Shen, H.; Zhang, H.; You, X. An enhanced SCMA detector enabled by deep neural network. In Proceedings of the 2018 IEEE/CIC International Conference on Communications in China (ICCC), Beijing, China, 16–18 August 2018; pp. 835–839.
77. Tsai, C.H.; Lin, K.H.; Wei, H.Y.; Yeh, F.M. QoE-aware Q-learning based approach to dynamic TDD uplink-downlink reconfiguration in indoor small cell networks. *Wirel. Netw.* **2019**, *25*, 3467–3479. [CrossRef]
78. Wang, D.; Khosla, A.; Gargeya, R.; Irshad, H.; Beck, A.H. Deep learning for identifying metastatic breast cancer. *arXiv* **2016**, arXiv:1606.05718.
79. Kachuee, M.; Fazeli, S.; Sarrafzadeh, M. Ecg heartbeat classification: A deep transferable representation. In Proceedings of the 2018 IEEE International Conference on Healthcare Informatics (ICHI), New York, NY, USA, 4–7 June 2018; pp. 443–444.
80. Patil, K.; Kulkarni, M.; Sriraman, A.; Karande, S. Deep learning based car damage classification. In Proceedings of the 2017 16th IEEE International Conference on Machine Learning and Applications (ICMLA), Cancun, Mexico, 18–21 December 2017; pp. 50–54.
81. Song, Q.; Zhao, L.; Luo, X.; Dou, X. Using deep learning for classification of lung nodules on computed tomography images. *J. Healthc. Eng.* **2017**, *2017*, 1–7. [CrossRef]
82. Kendall, A.; Cipolla, R. Geometric loss functions for camera pose regression with deep learning. In Proceedings of the IEEE Conference on Computer Vision and Pattern Recognition, Honolulu, HI, USA, 21–26 July 2017; pp. 5974–5983.
83. Liu, C.; Wang, Z.; Wu, S.; Wu, S.; Xiao, K. Regression Task on Big Data with Convolutional Neural Network. In Proceedings of the International Conference on Advanced Machine Learning Technologies and Applications, Cairo, Egypt, 28–30 March 2019; pp. 52–58.
84. Maqueda, A.I.; Loquercio, A.; Gallego, G.; García, N.; Scaramuzza, D. Event-based vision meets deep learning on steering prediction for self-driving cars. In Proceedings of the IEEE Conference on Computer Vision and Pattern Recognition, Salt Lake City, UT, USA, 18–23 June 2018; pp. 5419–5427.
85. Fahrettin Koyuncu, C.; Gunesli, G.N.; Cetin-Atalay, R.; Gunduz-Demir, C. DeepDistance: A Multi-task Deep Regression Model for Cell Detection in Inverted Microscopy Images. *arXiv* **2019**, arXiv:1908.11211.
86. Arulkumaran, K.; Deisenroth, M.P.; Brundage, M.; Bharath, A.A. A brief survey of deep reinforcement learning. *arXiv* **2017**, arXiv:1708.05866.
87. Zaheer, M.; Ahmed, A.; Smola, A.J. Latent LSTM allocation joint clustering and non-linear dynamic modeling of sequential data. In Proceedings of the 34th International Conference on Machine Learning, Sydney, Australia, 6–11 August 2017; Volume 70, pp. 3967–3976.

88. Niu, D.; Liu, Y.; Cai, T.; Zheng, X.; Liu, T.; Zhou, S. A Novel Distributed Duration-Aware LSTM for Large Scale Sequential Data Analysis. In Proceedings of the CCF Conference on Big Data, Wuhan, China, 26–28 September 2019; pp. 120–134.
89. Yildirim, Ö. A novel wavelet sequence based on deep bidirectional LSTM network model for ECG signal classification. *Comput. Biol. Med.* **2018**, *96*, 189–202. [CrossRef] [PubMed]
90. Greff, K.; Srivastava, R.K.; Koutník, J.; Steunebrink, B.R.; Schmidhuber, J. LSTM: A search space odyssey. *IEEE Trans. Neural Netw. Learn. Syst.* **2016**, *28*, 2222–2232. [CrossRef]
91. Bai, S.; Kolter, J.Z.; Koltun, V. An empirical evaluation of generic convolutional and recurrent networks for sequence modeling. *arXiv* **2018**, arXiv:1803.01271.
92. Jiang, M.; Liang, Y.; Feng, X.; Fan, X.; Pei, Z.; Xue, Y.; Guan, R. Text classification based on deep belief network and softmax regression. *Neural Comput. Appl.* **2018**, *29*, 61–70. [CrossRef]
93. Barlacchi, G.; De Nadai, M.; Larcher, R.; Casella, A.; Chitic, C.; Torrisi, G.; Antonelli, F.; Vespignani, A.; Pentland, A.; Lepri, B. A multi-source dataset of urban life in the city of Milan and the Province of Trentino. *Sci. Data* **2015**, *2*, 150055. [CrossRef]
94. Garcia, S.; Grill, M.; Stiborek, J.; Zunino, A. An empirical comparison of botnet detection methods. *Comput. Secur.* **2014**, *45*, 100–123. [CrossRef]
95. Raca, D.; Quinlan, J.J.; Zahran, A.H.; Sreenan, C.J. Beyond throughput: A 4G LTE dataset with channel and context metrics. In Proceedings of the 9th ACM Multimedia Systems Conference, Amsterdam, The Netherlands, 12–15 June 2018; pp. 460–465.
96. Borges, V.C.; Cardoso, K.V.; Cerqueira, E.; Nogueira, M.; Santos, A. Aspirations, challenges, and open issues for software-based 5G networks in extremely dense and heterogeneous scenarios. *EURASIP J. Wirel. Commun. Netw.* **2015**, *2015*, 1–13. [CrossRef]
97. Ge, X.; Li, Z.; Li, S. 5G software defined vehicular networks. *IEEE Commun. Mag.* **2017**, *55*, 87–93. [CrossRef]
98. Ye, H.; Liang, L.; Li, G.Y.; Kim, J.; Lu, L.; Wu, M. Machine learning for vehicular networks: Recent advances and application examples. *IEEE Veh. Technol. Mag.* **2018**, *13*, 94–101. [CrossRef]
99. Li, S.; Da Xu, L.; Zhao, S. 5G Internet of Things: A survey. *J. Ind. Inf. Integr.* **2018**, *10*, 1–9. [CrossRef]
100. Kusume, K.; Fallgren, M.; Queseth, O.; Braun, V.; Gozalvez-Serrano, D.; Korthals, I.; Zimmermann, G.; Schubert, M.; Hossain, M.; Widaa, A.; et al. Updated scenarios, requirements and KPIs for 5G mobile and wireless system with recommendations for future investigations. In *Mobile and Wireless Communications Enablers for the Twenty-Twenty Information Society (METIS) Deliverable, ICT-317669-METIS D*; METIS: Stockholm, Sweden, 2015; Volume 1.

© 2020 by the authors. Licensee MDPI, Basel, Switzerland. This article is an open access article distributed under the terms and conditions of the Creative Commons Attribution (CC BY) license (http://creativecommons.org/licenses/by/4.0/).

Article

Safe Approximation—An Efficient Solution for a Hard Routing Problem

András Faragó and Zohre R. Mojaveri *

Department of Computer Science, Erik Jonsson School of Engineering and Computer Science, The University of Texas at Dallas, P.O.B. 830688, MS-EC31, Richardson, TX 75080, USA; farago@utdallas.edu
* Correspondence: zohre.r.mojaveri@utdallas.edu

Abstract: The *Disjoint Connecting Paths* problem and its capacitated generalization, called *Unsplittable Flow* problem, play an important role in practical applications such as communication network design and routing. These tasks are **NP**-hard in general, but various polynomial-time approximations are known. Nevertheless, the approximations tend to be either too loose (allowing large deviation from the optimum), or too complicated, often rendering them impractical in large, complex networks. Therefore, our goal is to present a solution that provides a relatively simple, efficient algorithm for the unsplittable flow problem in large directed graphs, where the task is **NP**-hard, and is known to remain **NP**-hard even to approximate up to a large factor. The efficiency of our algorithm is achieved by sacrificing a small part of the solution space. This also represents a novel paradigm for approximation. Rather than giving up the search for an *exact* solution, we restrict the solution space to a subset that is the most important for applications, and excludes only a small part that is marginal in some well-defined sense. Specifically, the sacrificed part only contains scenarios where some edges are very close to saturation. Since nearly saturated links are undesirable in practical applications, therefore, excluding near saturation is quite reasonable from the practical point of view. We refer the solutions that contain no nearly saturated edges as *safe solutions*, and call the approach *safe approximation*. We prove that this safe approximation can be carried out efficiently. That is, once we restrict ourselves to safe solutions, we can find the *exact* optimum by a randomized polynomial time algorithm.

Citation: Faragó, A.; Mojaveri, Z.R. Safe Approximation: An Efficient Solution for a Hard Routing Problem. *Algorithms* **2021**, *14*, 48. https://doi.org/10.3390/a14020048

Academic Editor: Andras Farago
Received: 8 December 2020
Accepted: 28 January 2021
Published: 2 February 2021

Publisher's Note: MDPI stays neutral with regard to jurisdictional claims in published maps and institutional affiliations.

Copyright: © 2021 by the authors. Licensee MDPI, Basel, Switzerland. This article is an open access article distributed under the terms and conditions of the Creative Commons Attribution (CC BY) license (https://creativecommons.org/licenses/by/4.0/).

Keywords: routing; **NP**-complete; **NP**-hard; approximation; polynomial time algorithm; disjoint connecting paths; unsplittable flow; network design

1. Introduction

In communication network design and routing, one often looks for disjoint routes that connect various sources with associated terminals. This motivates the Disjoint Connecting Paths problem, which is the following decision task:

Input: a set of source-destination node pairs $(s_1, t_1), \ldots, (s_k, t_k)$ in a graph.
Task: Find edge disjoint paths $P_1, \ldots, P_k$, such that P_i connects s_i with t_i for each i.

This is one of the classical **NP**-complete problems that appears already at the sources of **NP**-completess theory, among the original problems of Karp [1]. It remains **NP**-complete both for directed and undirected graphs, as well as for the edge disjoint and vertex disjoint paths version. The corresponding natural optimization problem, when we are looking for the maximum number of terminator pairs that can be connected by disjoint paths is **NP**-hard.

There is also a capacitated version of the Disjoint Connecting Paths problem, also known as the *Unsplittable Flow problem*. In this task a *flow demand* is given for each origin-destination pair (s_i, t_i), as well as a capacity value is known for each edge. The requirement is to find a system of paths, connecting the respective source-destination pairs and carrying the respective flow demands, such that the *capacity constraint* of each edge is obeyed, that is, the sum of the flows of paths that traverse the edge cannot be more than the capacity of the edge. The name *Unsplittable Flow* expresses the requirement that between each source-destination pair the flow must follow a single route, it cannot split. Note that the disjointness of the paths themselves is not required *a priori* in the Unsplittable Flow, but can be enforced by the capacity constraints, if needed. The Unsplittable Flow problem is widely regarded as a fundamental task in communication network design and routing applications. Note that it directly subsumes the Disjoint Connecting Paths problem as a special case, which can be obtained by taking all capacities and flow demands equal to 1.

In this paper, after reviewing some existing results, we show that the Unsplittable Flow problem, which is known to be **NP**-hard (and its decision version is **NP**-complete), becomes efficiently solvable if we impose a mild and practically well justifiable restriction. Specifically, our key idea is that we "cut down" a small part of the solution space by slightly reducing the edge capacities. In other words, we exclude solutions that are close to saturating some edges, which would be practically undesirable, anyway. We call remaining solutions *safe solutions*: safe in the sense that no link is very close to saturation. Why is this slight capacity reduction useful? Its usefulness is based on the fact, which we constructively prove in the paper, that if we restrict ourselves to safe solutions only, then the hard algorithmic problem becomes solvable by a relatively simple randomized polynomial time algorithm. With very high probability the algorithm finds the *exact optimum* in polynomial time, whenever there exists a safe solution. We call this approach *safe approximation*.

2. Previous Results

Considerable work was done on the Disjoint Connecting Paths problem, since its first appearance as an **NP**-complete task in the classic paper of Karp [1] in 1972.

One direction of research deals with finding the "heart" of the difficulty—the simplest restricted cases that still remain **NP**-complete. (Or **NP**-hard if the optimization version is considered, where we look for the maximum number of connecting paths, allowing that possibly not all source-destination pairs will be connected). Kramer and van Leeuwen [2] proves, motivated by VLSI layout design, that the problem remains **NP**-complete even for graphs as regular as a two dimensional mesh. If we restrict ourselves to undirected planar graphs with each vertex having degree at most three, the problem also remains **NP**-complete, as proven by Middendorf and Pfeiffer [3]. The optimization version remains **NP**-hard for trees with parallel edges, although there the decision problem is already solvable in polynomial time [4].

The restriction that we only allow paths which connect each source node with a *dedicated* target is essential. If this is relaxed and we are satisfied with edge disjoint paths that connect each source s_i with *some* of destinations t_j but not necessarily with t_i, then the problem becomes solvable with classical network flow techniques. Thus, the prescribed matching of sources and destinations causes a dramatic change in the problem complexity. Interestingly, it becomes already **NP**-complete if we require that just *one* of the sources is connected to a dedicated destination, the rest is relaxed as above (Faragó [5]).

Another group of results produces polynomial time algorithmic solutions for finding the paths, possibly using randomization, in *special classes* of graphs. For example, Middendorf and Pfeiffer [3] proves the following. Let us represent the terminator pairs by *demand edges*. These are additional edges that connect a source with its destination. If this extended graph is embeddable in the plane such that the demand edges lie in a bounded number of faces of the original graph, then the problem is solvable in polynomial time. (The faces are the planar regions bordered by the curves that represent the edges in the planar embedding, that is, in drawing the graph in the plane). Thus, this special case requires that, beyond the planarity of the extended graph, the terminators are concentrated in a constant number of regions (independent of the graph size), rather than spreading over the graph.

Broder, Frieze, Suen and Upfal [6] consider the case of *random graphs* and provide a randomized algorithm that, under some technical conditions, finds a solution with high probability in time $O(nm^2)$ for a random graph of n vertices and m edges.

A deep theoretical result, due to Robertson and Seymour [7], is that for general undirected graphs the problem can be solved in polynomial time if the number k of paths to be found is *constant* (i.e., cannot grow with the size of the graph). This is important from the theoretical point of view, but does not lead to a practical algorithm, as analyzed by Bienstock and Langston [8]. On the other hand, for directed graphs the problem becomes **NP**-complete already for the smallest nontrivial case of $k = 2$, as proven by Even, Itai, and Shamir [9].

Another line of research aims at finding approximations to the optimization version. An algorithm is said to be an $f(n)$-approximation if it can connect a subset of the terminator pairs by disjoint paths such that this subset is at most $f(n)$ times smaller than the optimum in a graph of n vertices. For example, in this terminology a 2-approximation algorithm always reaches at least the half of the optimum, or an $O(\log n)$-approximation reaches at least a $c/\log n$ fraction of the optimum, for $n > n_0$ with some constants c, n_0.

Various approximations have been presented in the literature. For example, Garg, Vazirani and Yannakakis [4] provide a 2-approximation for trees with parallel edges. Aumann and Rabani [10] gives an $O(\log n)$-approximation for the 2-dimensional mesh. Kleinberg and Tardos [11] present an $O(\log n)$-approximation for a larger subclass of planar graphs, they call "nearly Eulerian, uniformly high-diameter planar graphs."

On the other hand, finding a constant factor, or at least a logarithmic factor approximation for general directed graphs is hopeless—Guruswami, Khanna, Rajaraman, Shepherd, and Yannakakis [12] showed that on directed graphs it is **NP**-hard to obtain an $O(n^{1/2-\epsilon})$ approximation for n-vertex graphs for any $\epsilon > 0$.

For the general case the approximation factor of $\min\{\sqrt{m}, m/opt\} = O(\sqrt{m})$ is known to be achievable (Srinivasan [13]), where m is the number of edges and opt is the optimum, that is, the maximum number of disjoint connecting paths between the source-destination pairs. Similar bounds apply for the Unsplittable Flow problem, as well. Bounds have been also found in terms of special (less trivial) graph parameters. For example, Kolman and Scheideler [14] proves that an efficient $O(F)$ approximation exists, where F is the so called *flow number* of the graph. Although the flow number can be computed in polynomial time [14], it is a rather indirect characterization of the graph. Numerous further related results are reviewed in the Handbook of Approximation Algorithms and Metaheuristics [15].

It is worth noting that in the capacitated version (Unsplittable Flow problem) the approximation does *not* mean approximating the total carried flow. It is meant with respect to the number of source-destination pairs connected, such that for each pair their entire demand is carried. For example, if there are 30 source-destination pairs, each with flow demand four units, then a 2-approximation means routing at least 15 of these flows, each path carrying four units of flow. In other words, not only the paths are unsplittable, but also the flow demands. That is, if we connect all 30 source-destination pairs, but each route can carry only two units of flow, it would not count as a 2-approximation.

In summary, the landscape of the Disjoint Connecting Path and the Unsplittable Flow problems can be characterized by the following facts:

- The decision problems are **NP**-complete for the general case.
- The approximation versions are **NP**-hard for the general case, even within a large approximation factor.
- Polynomial time solutions or better approximations exist only for special cases.
- Even in those cases when a polynomial time solution exists, it is either far from practical, or else it applies to a graph class that is too special to satisfy the demands of network design applications.

3. The Method of Safe Approximation

The various above referenced solutions tend to be rather complicated, which is certainly not helpful for real-life applications, in particular for large, complex networks. Our approach for providing a more practical solution to the unsplittable flow problem based on the following idea. We "cut down" a small part of the solution space by slightly reducing the edge capacities. In other words, we exclude solutions that are close to saturating some edges, as explained below.

Let V_i be the given flow demand of the ith connecting path. We normalize these demands such that $V_i \leq 1$ for every i. Let C_j be the capacity of edge j. The graph is assumed directed and the edges are numbered from 1 through m. Recall that a feasible solution of the problem is a set of $s_i - t_i$ (directed) paths, one for each i, satisfying the edge capacity constraints. The latter means that on each edge j the sum of the V_i values of those paths that traverse the edge does not exceed C_j. As mentioned earlier, deciding whether a feasible solution exist at all is a hard (**NP**-complete) problem.

On the other hand, not all feasible solutions are equally good from a practical viewpoint. For example, if a route system in a network saturates or nearly saturates some links, then it is not preferable because it is close to being overloaded. For this reason, let us assign a parameter $0 < \rho_j < 1$ to each edge j, such that ρ_j will act as a *safety margin* for the edge. More precisely, let us call a feasible solution a *safe solution* with parameters ρ_j, $j = 1, \ldots, m$, where m is the number of edges, if it uses at most $\tilde{C}_j = \rho_j C_j$ capacity on edge j. The parameter ρ_j will be close to 1 in the cases that are interesting to us.

Now, the appealing thing is that if we restrict ourselves to only those cases when a safe solution exists, then the hard algorithmic problem becomes solvable by a relatively simple randomized polynomial time algorithm. With very high probability, the algorithm finds the *exact optimum* in polynomial time, whenever there exists a safe solution. We call this approach *safe approximation*.

The price is that we exclude those cases when a *feasible* solution might still possibly exists, but there is no *safe* solution. This means, in these cases all feasible solutions are undesirable, because they all make some edges nearly saturated. In these marginal cases the algorithm may find no solution at all. Our approach constitutes a new avenue to approximation, in the sense that instead of giving up finding an exact solution, we rather restrict the search space to a (slightly) smaller one. When, however, the algorithm finds *any* solution, then it provides the *exact* (not just approximate) optimum.

Let us choose the *safety margin* ρ_j for edge j in a graph of m edges as

$$\rho_j = 1 - (e-1)\sqrt{\frac{\ln 2m}{C_j}} \approx 1 - 1.71 \sqrt{\frac{\ln 2m}{C_j}}, \qquad (1)$$

where C_j is the capacity of edge j, ln denotes the natural logarithm $\log_e$, and $e \approx 2.718\ldots$ is Euler's number (the base of the natural logarithm). Note that ρ_j tends to 1 with growing C_j, even if the graph also grows, but C_j grows faster than the logarithm of the graph size, which is very reasonable (note that doubling the number of edges will only increase the natural logarithm by less than 1). For example, if an edge has capacity $C_j = 1000$ units (measured in relative units, such that the maximum path flow demand is 1), and the graph has $m = 200$ edges, then $\rho_j \approx 0.87$.

Now, we outline how the algorithm works. First, we describe a continuous multicommodity flow relaxation.

Continuous multicommodity flow relaxation Let V_i be the given flow demand of the ith connecting path, with source node s_i and target node t_i. We refer to i as the *type* of the flow. For each such type, and for each edge j, assign a non-negative variable x^i_j, representing the amount of type-i flow on edge j. The flow model is then expressed by the following constraints:

1. **Capacity constraints** For every edge j

$$\sum_i x^i_j \leq \rho_j C_j. \qquad (2)$$

The meaning of (2) is that the flow on edge j, summed over all types, cannot be more than the capacity of the edge, reduced by the safety margin.

2. **Flow conservation** For every node v, let $\text{In}(v)$ denote the set of incoming edges of v. Similarly, let $\text{Out}(v)$ be the set of outgoing edges of v. Then write for every flow type i and for every node v, except s_i and t_i:

$$\sum_{j \in \text{In}(v)} x_j^i = \sum_{k \in \text{Out}(v)} x_k^i. \qquad (3)$$

The meaning of (3) is that for every flow type i, the type-i flow is conserved at every node, except its source s_i and destination t_i. By conservation we mean that the total incoming type-i flow to v is equal to the total outgoing type-i flow from v.

3. **Source constraints** For every flow type i (which has its source at node s_i):

$$\sum_{j \subset \text{Out}(s_i)} x_j^i = V_i. \qquad (4)$$

The meaning of (4) is that source s_i should emit V_i amount of type-i flow.

Now we can describe our algorithm. The used notations are summarized in Table 1.

Table 1. Notations and Definitions.

Notations	Definitions
m	Number of edges
n	Number of verticies
V_i	Given flow demand of the ith connecting path
s_i	Source node
t_i	Target node
p_j	Safety margin of edge j
v	Node
$\text{In}(v)$	Set of incoming edges of v
$\text{Out}(v)$	Set of outgoing edges of v
F_j	Flow (=expected load) on edge j
X_i	A random variable
i	Type of the flow
j, k	Edge
x_j^i	Non-negative variable representing the amount of type-i flow on edge j
C_j	Capacity of edge j
k	Path

Procedure

Step 1 *Multicommodity flow relaxation*
Solve the following linear program:

$$\min \sum_i \sum_j x_j^i \qquad (5)$$

Subject to

$$\sum_i x_j^i \leq p_j C_j \qquad (\forall j)$$

$$\sum_{j \in \text{In}(v)} x_j^i = \sum_{k \in \text{Out}(v)} x_k^i \qquad (\forall i, \forall v \neq s_i, t_i)$$

$$\sum_{j \in \text{Out}(s_i)} x_j^i = V_i \qquad (\forall i)$$

$$x_j^i \geq 0 \qquad (\forall i, j).$$

In case there is no feasible solution, then declare "no safe solution exists" and HALT.

Step 2 *Path Creation via Random Walk*
For each source-destination pair s_i, t_i find a path via the following randomized procedure. Start at the source s_i and take the next node such that it is drawn randomly among the successor neighbors of the source, with probabilities proportional to the ith commodity flow values on the edges from s_i to the successor neighbors in the directed graph. Continue this in a similar manner—at each node choose the next one among its successor neighbors randomly, with probabilities that are proportional to the ith commodity flow values. Finally, upon arrival at t_i, we store the found (s_i, t_i) path.

Step 3 *Feasibility Check and Repetition*
Having found a system of paths in the previous step, check whether it is a feasible solution (i.e., it can carry the flow demand for each path within the capacity bounds). If so, then HALT, else repeat from Step 2.
If after repeating r times (r is a fixed parameter) none of the runs are successful then declare "No solution is found" and HALT.

It is clear from the above description that the algorithm has practically feasible complexity, since the most complex part is the linear programming. Note that while Step 2 is repeated r times, the linear program in Step 1 needs to be solved only once. The correctness of the algorithm is shown in the following theorem.

Theorem 1. *If a safe solution exists, then the algorithm finds a feasible solution with probability at least $1 - 2^{-r}$.*

Proof. Since a safe solution is also a feasible solution of the multicommodity flow relaxation, therefore, if there is no flow solution in Step 1, then no safe solution can exist either.

Step 2 transforms the flow solution into paths. To see that they are indeed paths, observe that looping cannot occur in the randomized branching procedure, because if a circle arises on the way, that would mean a circle with all positive flow values for a given commodity, which could be canceled from the flow of that commodity, thus contradicting to the fact that the linear program finds a flow in which the sum of edge flows is minimum, according to the objective function (5). Furthermore, since looping cannot occur, we must reach the destination via the procedure in at most n steps, where n is the number of nodes.

Now a key observation is that if we build the paths with the described randomization between the ith source-destination pair, then the *expected value* of the load that is put on any given edge by these paths will be exactly the value of the ith commodity flow on the link. This follows from the fact that the branching probabilities are flow-proportional.

From the above we know that the total expected load of an edge, arising form the randomly chosen paths, is equal to the total flow value on the edge. What we have to bound is the deviation of the *actual* load from this expected value. Let F_j be the flow (=expected load) on edge j. This arises in the randomized procedure as

$$F_j = E\left(\sum_i V_i X_i\right), \tag{6}$$

where X_i is a random variable that takes the value 1 if the ith path (i.e., the type-i flow) contributes to the edge load, otherwise it is 0. The construction implies that these random variables are independent, whenever j is a fixed edge and i runs over the different flow types.

Now consider the random variable

$$\Psi_j = \sum_i V_i X_i.$$

By (6), we have $E(\Psi_j) = F_j$. The probability that the actual random value Ψ_j deviates form its expected value by F_j by more than a factor of δ can be bounded by the tail inequality found in [16], which is a variant of the Chernoff-Hoeffding bound:

$$\Pr\left(\Psi_j > (1+\delta)F_j\right) < \left(\frac{e^\delta}{(1+\delta)^{(1+\delta)}}\right)^{F_j}.$$

It can be calculated from this [16] that if we want to guarantee that the bound does not exceed a given value $\epsilon > 0$, then it is sufficient to satisfy

$$\delta \leq (e-1)\sqrt{\frac{\ln(1/\epsilon)}{F_j}}.$$

Let us choose $\epsilon = 1/(2m)$. Then we have

$$\Pr\left(\Psi_j > \underbrace{\left(1+(e-1)\sqrt{\frac{\ln(1/\epsilon)}{F_j}}\right)F_j}_{\delta}\right) < \frac{1}{2m}.$$

Since the bound that we do not want to exceed is the edge capacity C_j, therefore, if

$$C_j \geq \left(1+(e-1)\sqrt{(\ln 2m)/F_j}\right)F_j \quad (7)$$

is satisfied, then we have

$$\Pr(\Psi_j > C_j) < \frac{1}{2m}.$$

If this holds for all edges, it yields

$$\Pr(\exists j : \Psi_j > C_j) \leq \sum_{j=1}^{m} \Pr(\Psi_j > C_j)$$
$$< m \cdot \frac{1}{2m}$$
$$= \frac{1}{2}.$$

Thus, the probability that the found path system is not feasible is less than $1/2$. Repeating the procedure r times with independent randomness, the probability that none of the trials provide a feasible solution is bounded by $1/2^r$, that is, the failure probability becomes very small, already for moderate values of r.

Finally, expressing F_j form (7) we obtain

$$F_j \leq C_j\left(1-(e-1)\sqrt{\frac{\ln 2m}{C_j}}\right) = \rho_j C_j,$$

which shows that the safety margin is correctly chosen, thus completing the proof. □

4. Simulation Experiments

We have carried out simulation experiments to demonstrate how our approach performs in practice. Below we summarize the experimental results.

The calculation of the safety margin ρ for the edges is based on formula (1). Note that the safety margin is determined by the number of edges and the edge capacities, and the meaning of the safety margin is the fraction of the maximum edge capacity that can be used by our algorithm. This is shown in Table 2, for edge numbers running from 20 through 800, and with edge capacities 1000 and 2000. For example, the second line in the table shows that for 20 edges and capacities of 2000 units the resulting safety margin is 0.926 (92.6%), which allows the usage of 1852 units of capacity, out of 2000 units. The content of Table 2 is represented graphically in Figure 1.

Table 2. Capacity constraints of edges with different safety margin.

No. of Edges m	Capacity of Edges	Safety Margin for Edges	Capacity Constraints
20	1000	0.896	896
20	2000	0.926	1852
200	1000	0.867	867
200	2000	0.906	1812
400	1000	0.86	860
400	2000	0.901	1802
600	1000	0.856	856
600	2000	0.898	1796
800	1000	0.853	853
800	2000	0.896	1792

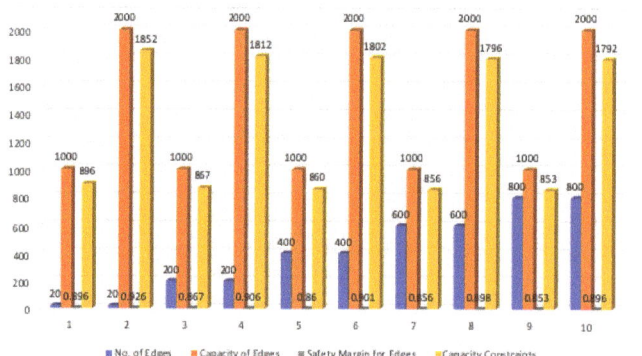

Figure 1. Safety margin and capacity constraints for edges.

In our simulation experiments, the number of nodes ranges from 5 to 40, while the number of edges ranges from 7 through 62. The actual graph (network topology) is chosen randomly. An example is shown in Figure 2. For each number of edges we ran the simulation with two different edge capacities: $C = 1000$ and $C = 2000$ units. As the safety margin increases with higher capacities, the network can be better utilized, since the safety margin determines what percentage of the maximum capacity is utilized.

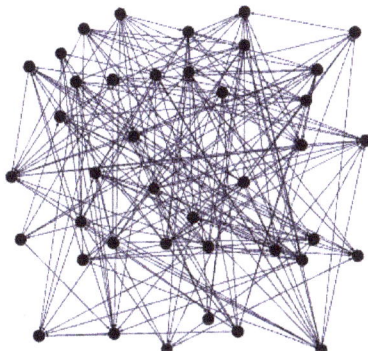

Figure 2. A sample network topology.

We ran the simulation with two different traffic types (two commodities in the multi-commodity flow); they represent two source-terminal pairs, which were chosen randomly. Furthermore, the number of nodes and edges were varied: the nodes between 5 and 40, the edges between 7 and 62. The results are shown in Table 3. The table contains that for various numbers of nodes and edges, how many iterations were needed to find the optimum, and what was the optimum objective function value in terms of total carried traffic. The same results are represented graphically in Figure 3. The results allowed us to make some observations:

- As the number of nodes and edges increase, that is, the network becomes larger, the algorithm tends to require more iterations to find the optimum, which, of course, is not surprising.
- By setting the repetition parameter to $r = 8$, the algorithm returned an optimal solution in 100% of the cases, which is very encouraging. It shows that one does not need an astronomical number of iterations to guarantee the optimum.
- In some cases (actually 25% the of all cases we tried) already the first iteration achieved the optimum. Furthermore, in 75% of cases at most 5 iterations were sufficient to reach the optimum, and we never needed more than 8. Of course, these are relatively small examples, but it reinforces the observation that a limited number of iterations suffice.

Table 3. Simulation results.

No. of Nodes n	No. of Edges m	Solved in Iteration r	Optimal Objective
5	7	2	550×10^3
10	15	1	1.100×10^3
15	22	1	1.650×10^3
20	30	4	2.200×10^3
25	39	5	2.750×10^3
30	46	5	3.300×10^3
35	54	6	3.850×10^3
40	62	8	4.400×10^3

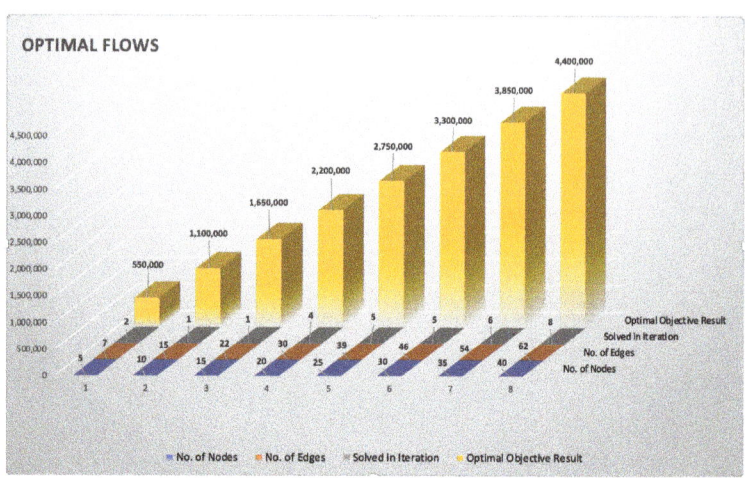

Figure 3. Optimal flows of packet traffic.

5. Conclusions

We have presented an efficient solution for the **NP**-complete Unsplittable Flow problem in directed graphs. The efficiency is achieved by sacrificing a small part of the solution space. The sacrificed part only contains scenarios where some edges are close to saturation, which is undesired in practical applications, anyway. The solutions that exclude such nearly saturated edges are called *safe solutions*.

The approach constitutes a new avenue to approximation, which we call *safe approximation*. It means that instead of giving up the exact solution, we rather restrict the search space to a (slightly) smaller one. When, however, the algorithm finds any solution, which happens with very high probability, then it is an *exact* (not just an approximate) solution.

Author Contributions: Writing—original draft, A.F.; writing—review and editing, creating the simulation and drawing figures, Z.R.M. All authors have read and agreed to the published version of the manuscript.

Funding: This research received no external funding.

Conflicts of Interest: The authors declare no conflict of interest.

References

1. Karp, R.M. Reducibility Among Combinatorial Problems. In *Complexity of Computer Computations*; Miller, R.E., Thatcher, J.W., Eds.; Plenum Press: New York, NY, USA, 1972.
2. Kramer, M.E.; van Leeuwen, J. The Complexity of Wire Routing and Finding the Minimum Area Layouts for Arbitrary VLSI Circuits. In *Advances in Computing Research 2: VLSI Theory*; Preparata, F., Ed.; JAI Press: London, UK, 1984.
3. Middendorf, M.; Pfeiffer, F. On the Complexity of the Disjoint Paths Problem. In *Polyhedral Combinatorics*; Cook, W., Seymour, P.D., Eds.; DIMACS Series in Discrete Mathematics and Theoretical Computer Science; American Mathematical Society: Providence, RI, USA, 1990.
4. Garg, N.; Vazirani, V.; Yannakakis, M. Primal-Dual Approximation Algorithms for Integral Flow and Multicuts in Trees, with Applications to Matching and Set Cover. In *International Colloquium on Automata, Languages, and Programming*; Springer: Berlin/Heidelberg, Germany, 1993; pp. 64–75.
5. Faragó, A. Algorithmic Problems in Graph Theory. In *Conference of Program Designers*; Eötvös Loránd University of Sciences: Budapest, Hungary, 1985; pp. 61–66.
6. Broder, A.A.; Frieze, A.M.; Suen, S.; Upfal, E. Optimal Construction of Edge-Disjoint Paths in Random Graphs. In Proceedings of the ACM-SIAM Symposium on Discrete Algorithms (SODA), Arlington, VA, USA, 23–25 January 1994; pp. 603–612.
7. Robertson, N.; Seymour, P.D. Graph Minors-XIII: The Disjoint Paths Problem. *J. Comb.* **1995**, *63*, 65–110. [CrossRef]
8. Bienstock, D.; Langston, M.A. Algorithmic implications of the Graph Minor Theorem. In *Handbook in Operations Research and Management Science 7: Network Models*; Ball, M.O., Magnanti, T.L., Monma, C.L., Nemhauser, G.L., Eds.; North-Hollandhl: Amsterdam, The Netherlands, 1995.

9. Even, S.; Itai, A.; Shamir, A. On the complexity of timetable and multicommodity flow problems. *SIAM J. Comput.* **1976**, *5*, 691–703. [CrossRef]
10. Aumann, Y.; Rabani, Y. Improved Bounds for All-Optical Routing. In Proceedings of the ACM-SIAM Symposium on Discrete Algorithms (SODA), San Francisco, CA, USA, 22–24 January 1995; pp. 567–576.
11. Kleinberg, J.; Tardos, É. Approximations for the Disjoint Paths Problem in High-Diameter Planar Networks. In Proceedings of the ACM Symposium on Theory of Computing (STOC'95), Las Vegas, NV, USA, 29 May–1 June 1995; pp. 26–35.
12. Guruswami, V.; Khanna, S.; Rajaraman, R.; Shepherd, B.; Yannakakis, M. Near-optimal hardness results and approximation algorithms for edge-disjoint paths and related problems. *J. Comput. Syst. Sci.* **2003**, *67*, 473–496. [CrossRef]
13. Srinivasan, A. Improved Approximations for Edge-disjoint Paths, Unsplittable Flow, and Related Routing Problems. In Proceedings of the 38th IEEE Symposium on Foundations of Computer Science (FOCS'97), Miami Beach, FL, USA, 19–22 October 1997; pp. 416–425.
14. Kolman, P.; Scheideler, C. Improved Bounds for the Unsplittable Flow Problem. *J. Algorithms* **2006**, *61*, 20–44. [CrossRef]
15. Gonzales, T. (Ed.) *Handbook of Approximation Algorithms and Metaheuristics*; Chapman and Hall/CRC: Boca Raton, FL, USA, 2020.
16. Raghavan, P. Probabilistic Construction of Deterministic Algorithms: Approximating Packing Integer Programs. *J. Comput. Syst. Sci.* **1988**, *37*, 130–143. [CrossRef]

Article

A Hybrid Metaheuristic Algorithm for the Efficient Placement of UAVs

Stephanie Alvarez Fernandez *, Marcelo M. Carvalho * and Daniel G. Silva *

Department of Electrical Engineering, University of Brasília, Brasília 70910-900, Brazil
* Correspondence: salvarez@unb.br (S.A.F.); mmcarvalho@ene.unb.br (M.M.C.); danielgs@ene.unb.br (D.G.S.)

Received: 30 September 2020; Accepted: 1 November 2020; Published: 3 December 2020

Abstract: This work addresses the problem of using Unmanned Aerial Vehicles (UAV) to deploy a wireless aerial relay communications infrastructure for stations scattered on the ground. In our problem, every station in the network must be assigned to a single UAV, which is responsible for handling all data transfer on behalf of the stations that are assigned to it. Consequently, the placement of UAVs is key to achieving both network coverage and the maximization of the aggregate link capacities between UAVs and stations, and among the UAVs themselves. Because the complexity of this problem increases significantly with the number of stations to cover, for a given fixed number p of available UAVs, we model it as a single allocation p-hub median optimization problem, and we propose a hybrid metaheuristic algorithm to solve it. A series of numerical experiments illustrate the efficiency of the proposed algorithm against traditional optimization tools, which achieves high-quality results in very short time intervals, thus making it an attractive solution for real-world application scenarios.

Keywords: unmanned aerial vehicles; UAV placement; metaheuristics

1. Introduction

Unmanned Aerial Vehicles (UAV), also known as remotely piloted aircraft, were initially used in military applications. Nevertheless, with the development of various technologies in the telecommunications industry, UAVs have become more affordable and accessible to civilian and commercial applications [1]. This has eased the use and allowed for the application of multiple UAVs in singular tasks, such as traffic control, cargo transport, emergency and rescue operations, weather monitoring, among others. In these tasks, it is expected that UAVs are enabled with communication resources in order to allow the exchange of information with other agents of the environment in a bidirectional way.

The use of UAVs in emergency and unexpected circumstances, such as disaster relief and service recovery, has become a focus of study, because the deployment of terrestrial infrastructure is economically infeasible or simply not doable. Compared to a single UAV, there are several advantages to establishing and using a system with multiple UAVs, which can be enumerated as follows [2]: (*i*) the purchase and maintenance of several small aircrafts is cheaper than a large UAV with a size equivalent to the group formed by small ones; (*ii*) the use of a large UAV scarcely increases the coverage area, whereas multiple UAVs increase the scalability of the operation easily, and (*iii*) in the event of UAV failure, the possibility of "survival" or continuity in the execution of a multi-UAV mission is much greater than in a mission in which the failing UAV is the only executor. Naturally, the deployment of an aerial networking infrastructure formed by multiple UAVs also brings about a number of challenges and potential disadvantages if compared to the use of a single UAV. In particular, aerial multi-hop communication introduces additional delays to packet flows due to a number of factors, such as (*i*) the typical store-and-forward operation of UAVs when relaying packets to each other; (*ii*) the mechanisms of the medium access control (MAC) protocol in place to share the wireless channel(s) and support reliable data transfer; (*iii*) packet buffering in all UAVs; and, (*iv*) distributed user association, authentication procedures, etc. Needless to say, other issues arise that are related to trust and security of many deployed UAVs [3,4].

In this work, we look at the problem of UAV-assisted wireless communications [5], where UAVs are deployed to establish an aerial communication platform to provide wireless access for terrestrial users from the sky. In other words, the deployed UAVs do not generate their own data packets. Instead, the UAVs simply serve as aerial relays to connect users on the ground. We consider that each station is assigned to a single UAV, which is responsible for carrying data traffic to or from users assigned to other UAVs. Hence, different from recent work in the literature, where the UAV placement problem seeks to maximize the number of covered users [6,7] or to minimize the number of required UAVs [8,9], our goal is to maximize the total (sum) link capacity of the aerial communication infrastructure (considering both air-to-ground (A2G) and air-to-air (A2A) link capacities) given a fixed number of UAVs that are placed at the same (given) altitude from the ground. For that, and in line with other works [6–11], perfect user location information (ULI) is assumed. Because of such constraints, there is no minimum link rate requirement in our problem, and the provisioning of connectivity to all users is of paramount importance. In this sense, the solution we provide is best suited to application scenarios related to disaster relief, rescue operations, and provisioning of user connectivity in remote or hostile environments, for example. We recognize the UAV placement problem at hands as a typical p-hub median problem, according to which the goal is to determine the location of p "facilities" in a network of n nodes, while the total "distance" between demanding nodes and the nearest facility is minimized. Given the well-known combinatorial complexity of this problem, we propose and analyze two optimization strategies: (*i*) the application of CPLEX's branch-and-cut optimizer (version 12.10.0) and (*ii*) the biased randomized-Iterated Local Search (BR-ILS) metaheuristic algorithm, which is capable of delivering close-to-optimal results under significant gains in computational time, with respect to the former method.

The rest of the paper is organized, as follows: Section 2 presents a review on related work; Section 3 presents the system model of the UAVs placement problem; Section 4 presents the methodology to solve the aforementioned problem; Section 5 reports the computational results; and, finally, Section 6 concludes with a summary and future research.

2. Related Work

Employing UAVs as aerial communication platforms has become a rising research topic. As mentioned before, UAV-aided wireless communications have found a wide range of applications during the last decade [12–15] and, more recently, many authors have addressed the placement problem. In particular, in [15], the authors dealt with the UAV placement problem with non-orthogonal multiple access techniques and proposed a machine learning approach in order to adjust the UAVs' positions within the three-dimensional space, when the ground users are roaming. The Q-learning-based algorithm was applied when UAVs were moving. The authors tested two different scenarios: a single UAV case considering three users that were uniformly distributed within an area of 1 km × 1 km, and a multiple-UAV case. Unfortunately, the work did not attempt to solve the problem for large network sizes. Besides, a unified spatial analytical approach for non-orthogonal-aided UAV networks is desired, as the authors themselves pointed out. The proposed machine learning framework left some open issues such as the time it takes the algorithm to be tested and the considerable delays if the number of users is large.

In [16], the authors proposed a minimax facility location model for optimizing network delays that are caused by topological arrangements, which occur during UAV deployment in heterogeneous networks, and their mapping to a particular demand area. Instead of considering data link rates, the proposed model was aimed in the direction of the delay optimization by accurate positioning of the UAVs. The authors solved the question using entropy nets, which the authors considered to be the neural network version of decision trees. In that approach, a decision is taken while using fewer neural connections. The proposed approach was tested in a network of up to 500 users and six UAVs in an area of 10 km × 10 km. Later, the same authors proposed a similar approach to overcome the two problems, namely, the Macro Base Station decision problem and the cooperative UAV allocation problem [17]. Howeber, the proposed approach proved to be time consuming and the delays varied with an increase of the size network, since more iterations were required to localize the additional UAVs.

In [18], the authors studied the deployment of a Software Defined Network (SDN)-based UAV network, where the UAVs act as forwarding elements and the SDN controller manages the network. In particular, the issue of control overhead caused by the UAV-SDN controller communication was discussed. Here, the authors have not considered the delay due to data link rates, but, due to multi-hop communication, the UAVs are interconnected and each control packet between UAVs and the SDN controller will be transmitted multiple times. The authors proposed a scheme involving the buffering of update packets at intermediate nodes and merging of control packets to achieve a trade-off between control overhead and delay. The authors tested the proposed scheme in a network with a total of 36 UAVs deployed in an 1 km × 1 km area, with the controller being placed at some specific corner. The simulations results have shown that, as buffering time increases, the delay increases, as expected, but overhead decreases.

In [19], the authors investigated the problem of positioning UAVs in a wireless ad hoc network. They modeled the problem as a facility location problem and proposed a quadratic unconstrained binary optimization model. The main objective was to improve the connectivity at the shortest total distance and to maximize the linkage (downlink). The problem was solved using CPLEX's branch-and-cut optimizer. Test problems of size $m = 10$ to 100 for the wireless nodes, and $n = 3$ to 7 for the UAVs were generated and solved. Despite the effort of the authors for solving different scenarios varying the number of users and UAVs, large networks were not considered. On the other hand, in [20], the authors proposed a relay placement mechanism in order to find the ideal location for UAVs that act as relay nodes, in order to support live video transmissions with satisfactory quality of experience to the users and improving the connectivity. The authors considered a flying ad hoc network scenario implemented on the Mobile MultiMedia Wireless Sensor Network (M3WSN) OMNeT++ framework [21] composed of 30 UAVs moving over an area of 150 m × 150 m. Although the results appear to be satisfactory in terms of maintaining network connectivity while supporting real time multimedia transmissions, the entire terrain scenario can be considered reasonably small.

In [22], the authors considered the final deployment location of an UAV facility in a three-dimensional space with the aim of reaching a balance between service quality and interference. The authors took different scenarios into account, where either each user is selfish, and prefers the UAV to be located as close to himself as possible, or not, and they proposed a strategy-proof mechanism to overcome this issue. The success of the mechanism depends on whether the users report their locations truthfully. The authors presented empirical analysis in a single UAV scenario. In [23], the authors addressed the mission assignment and location management for UAVs in a mission-critical flying ad hoc network. The authors considered a scenario where the origin node is the ground control station and the destination node is a mission-performing UAV. Thus, the model aims to find UAVs' optimal mission assignment and locations together by maximizing the weighted sum of the communication performance and the mission performance functions. They assumed that UAVs that are not assigned to any mission are operated as relay nodes. The authors considered the communication performance as the lowest channel capacity among the links belonging to routing paths. In order to evaluate the communication performance, the authors did not consider area or coverage nor delay or data link rates, instead they considered a function in terms of the mission assignments, the locations of all nodes and the routing protocol in use. They proposed a Particle Swarm Optimization algorithm in order to solve the joint problem. A simulation scenario with 7 to 20 available UAVs and two missions was considered.

In [24], the authors dealt with the UAV placement problem in a multi-channel UAV network, in order to be resilient to any device or link capability loss. The authors modeled the problem that was based on Coulumb's law, with users being represented as positive charges and drones as negative charges. In this model, UAVs are supposed to be attracted by users within their sensing range. By doing so, the authors focused on an initial UAV positioning in order to seek an optimal coverage. In the proposed model, the authors took into account the mean lifetime of the drones, the IEEE 802.11 communication protocol and the drones capacity. The proposal was evaluated with the help of a simulator developed by the authors, considering 500 users and up to 10 UAVs. The proposed framework was set up for particular events, such as a public gathering or a disaster situation where the network should be quickly deployed. However, the work failed to present numerical values regarding the time that is spent on finding a solution and the delay related to the data link rate.

More recently, in [25], the authors investigated the router node placement problem within a specific geographical area. The idea was to form a viable, UAV-composed, ad hoc wireless mesh network that has performance measures optimized via a rapidly exploring random trees-based algorithm. The authors proposed a model that uses network coverage as an objective function which asses the total geographical area covered by the wireless mesh network. The authors did not focus on the delay related to the data link rates but on the network connectivity; thus, they included a penalty function that evaluate how infeasible a particular solution is based on a distance measure. The authors considered three different cases consisting of 16, 32, and 200 mesh routers in areas of 32×32, 64×64, and $4000\,\text{m} \times 4000\,\text{m}$, respectively. The performance of the proposed algorithm was compared with two optimization techniques: Particle Swarm Optimization and covariance matrix adaptation evolution strategy; computation times at 20.1 s for large instances were presented.

Despite the efforts and methodologies that were proposed by many authors, there are still open questions that need to be answered in order to effectively solve the placement of UAVs. One concern is regarding the requirement of a more autonomous and quick response by current applications when deploying UAV networks. Another matter is related to the placement of UAVs in disaster scenarios. In such events, it is preferable to obtain solutions to UAV placement through algorithms that do not consume too much time. On the other hand, a framework for UAV networks that can be effortlessly changed to fit different network scenarios in terms of number of users and geographical area dimensions is desired. Moreover, the performance of an UAV network is usually measured in terms of network connectivity, which, in turn is focused on the distances between UAVs and users or delay due to propagation delay. However, data rate links play an important role when designing such networks and, therefore, the focus on the impact of this measure may help to design efficient placement of UAVs.

3. System Model and Problem Formulation

In this section, the problem of placing UAVs to build an aerial relay infrastructure for users scattered on the ground is modeled as a single allocation p-hub median problem [26]. The advantage of modeling the problem in this way is that we can limit the number of UAVs needed beforehand, which, in turn, can be adjusted depending of the size of the network. Moreover, by doing so, we consider UAV-ground and UAV-UAV channels. When considering these two types of channels, the UAV-aided communications exhibit several unique characteristics when compared to terrestrial communication networks [1]. In addition, we take network coverage at the expense of the overall increase in the link capacity of the network into account.

The p-hub median problem is a classic location problem in which the objective is to determine the placement of p facilities (called medians) in a graph of n nodes, that minimizes the sum of distances between each demanding node and the nearest median. Hence, the positioning of multiple UAVs as aerial relays can be regarded as a type of location problem if the individual nodes on the ground are seen as the clients (demanding nodes), while the UAVs are treated as the p medians providing a service (which, in our case, consists of relaying data packets to or from the nodes assigned to them).

As previously mentioned, perfect user location information is also assumed, and all UAVs must be placed at a fixed altitude h from the terrain (also defined beforehand). Due to these constraints and conditions, no minimum data link rate requirement is imposed, and the goal is to determine the placement of UAVs in the network so that the total (sum) link capacity is maximized, while every user on the ground is assigned to only one UAV.

3.1. The p-Median Optimization Problem

We use the quadratic integer programming formulation based on the very first model proposed by O'kelly [27], which has been extensively applied to solve small to large instances of p-hub median problems. Hence, before we apply it to the UAV-assisted communications infrastructure optimization problem, we first describe its general formulation according to the key variables, cost function, and optimization constraints.

The classical p-hub median problem consists of locating p hubs from a set of n nodes in such a way that the average distance between hubs and nodes is minimized. Thus, it is assumed that there is a set N of graph nodes, with cardinality $|N| = n$, which are respectively associated with two-dimensional (2D) coordinates (x, y), previously known. For every pair of users i and j, let W_{ij} represent "flow units" that need to be transferred from a source node i to a destination node j across either *one* or *two* hubs only. The cost of collecting W_{ij} units of flow from a source node i to a destination node j is denoted by T_{ij}. Given that we want to investigate whether a node i must (*i*) become one of the p hubs or (*ii*) be assigned (or not) to a given hub k, the decision variable is represented by X_{ik}, which is defined as

$$X_{ik} = \begin{cases} 1, & \text{if user } i \text{ is assigned to hub } k \\ 0, & \text{otherwise.} \end{cases}$$

The particular case $X_{kk} = 1$ means that user k has been *converted* into a hub. This is because the only locations that are searched to place the hubs are the positions of the users themselves. This means that, out of the n positions available, p of them will be occupied by a hub (i.e., a user will become a hub). Accordingly, the uncapacitated single allocation p-hub median problem can be formulated as follows:

$$\text{Minimize:} \quad \sum_{i,j,k,l \in N} W_{ij}(T_{ik}X_{ik} + T_{kl}X_{ik}X_{jl} + T_{jl}X_{jl}) \tag{1}$$

$$\text{Subject to:} \quad \sum_{k=1}^{n} X_{kk} = p, \tag{2}$$

$$\sum_{k=1}^{n} X_{ik} = 1, \quad \forall\, i \in N \tag{3}$$

$$X_{ik} \leq X_{kk}, \quad \forall\, i, k \in N \tag{4}$$

$$X_{ik} \in \{0, 1\}, \quad \forall\, i, k \in N \tag{5}$$

Equation (1) describes the cost function as the total sum transfer and transmission costs from origin user to its associated hub, between hubs, and from the destination hub to the destination user. Equation (2) gives the exact number of p hubs to be placed in the network. Equation (3) is the single allocation constraint, ensuring that the transmission from any source to user i and vice-versa, i.e., from user i to any destination node is only sent through the p-hub to which the user i is assigned. Equation (4) guarantees that a user cannot have a direct link to a node unless it is a hub, thus avoiding a direct path between origin and destination users and, finally, Equation (5) states that the decision variable must be binary (0 or 1).

The aforementioned equations summarize the problem, which is, finding the optimal locations of the p hubs (a subset of the nodes set), as well as the allocation of the remaining nodes to the hubs. This particular quadratic programming formulation has $\mathcal{O}(n^2)$ variables and it is hard to solve due to its non-convexity. Despite the possibility of conversion into a mixed integer linear program, it has been demonstrated that the linearization has $\mathcal{O}(n^3)$ variables and constraints, thus restricting the size of problems that may be solved [28,29].

3.2. System Model

In this section, we describe how we model the UAV placement problem as an uncapacitated single allocation p-hub median problem. We seek to find the locations of p UAVs that maximize the total (sum) link capacity, while ensuring that each of the n users are assigned to only one UAV, as mentioned before. Thus, because we target the application of the UAV-assisted relay infrastructure to scenarios, such as disaster relief, rescue operations, remote or hostile environments, etc., no minimum requirements are imposed on data link rates (i.e., we seek to provide the best possible data link rates under given circumstances). For that, we consider the Shannon capacity to express the maximum data rate (expressed in b/s) that can be achieved at either air-to-ground (A2G) or air-to-air (A2A) data link between two nodes i and k, i.e.,

$$C_{ik} = B \log_2 \left(1 + \frac{S_{ik}}{N}\right), \tag{6}$$

where B denotes the channel bandwidth (Hz), N is the noise power within the channel bandwidth B, and S_{ik} denotes the signal power received on either side of the A2G link (user i and UAV k), or in either side of the A2A link (UAV i and UAV k). In this scenario, the UAVs act as "base stations" to users on the ground, relaying data packets to or from any user assigned to it. Consequently, every transfer of data packets between a pair of users has to go through either two hops (one UAV assigned to both users) or three hops (two UAVs, each assigned to a distinct user in the pair). Additionally, the UAVs are responsible for the scheduling of all transmissions among users assigned to them, and they do so in a way that no interference occurs (i.e., all transmissions are assumed to be collision-free). Note that we are only concerned with establishing the aerial relay infrastructure by focusing on determining the optimal placement of UAVs that render the highest total (sum) rate capacity. Therefore, we do not consider flows of data packets between pairs of users, i.e., we are not concerned with data throughput in this work. This also means that signal interference due to the activity of other (distant) users or UAVs is not taken into account and, therefore, only thermal background noise is considered (assumed to be additive white Gaussian noise (AWGN)).

As far as the channel propagation model is concerned, we assume that all of the UAVs are placed at a constant altitude h from the ground (defined beforehand), and they are all in Line-of-Sight (LOS) to each other and to every other user on the ground. Consequently, the Friis path-loss propagation model is assumed [30] for both A2G and A2A channels, which means that the received signal power S_{ik} (in dBm) between a node i and a node k will be given by

$$S_{ik} = P_t + G_t + G_r - 20 \log_{10} \left(\frac{4\pi f_c}{c}\right) - 20 \log_{10}(d_{ik}), \tag{7}$$

where P_t is the transmit power (measured in dBm), G_t and G_r are the transmit and receive antenna gains, respectively (expressed in dBi), f_c is the carrier frequency (in Hz), c is the speed of ligth (3×10^8 m/s), and d_{ik} is the absolute distance (or LOS distance) between node i and node k. Thus, for an A2G link, the absolute distance between user i and UAV k will be given by $d_{ik} = \sqrt{h^2 + r_{ik}^2}$, where r_{ik} denotes the Euclidean distance between user i's location on the ground and the (x,y) coordinates of UAV k on the ground (i.e., its projection on the ground). Likewise, because all of the UAVs are located at the same altitude h, the absolute distance between UAV i and UAV k is simply given by $d_{ik} = r_{ik}$.

We first need to note that we are not dealing with specific flows of data packets between users in order to cast the problem of placing UAVs as aerial relays to users on the ground within the framework of a p-median optimization problem, as mentioned previously. Therefore, the term W_{ij} in Equation (1) simplifies to $W_{ij} = 1, \forall i, j \in N$. Moreover, because the problem formulation is posed as a minimization optimization problem, we consider the inverse of each link capacity as the corresponding link cost, i.e., the time needed to transmit a bit. Therefore, we let

$$T_{ij} = \frac{1}{C_{ij}} \qquad (8)$$

to express the link cost between node i and node j, i.e., a link either connecting a user i to an UAV j (A2G link), or an UAV i to an UAV j (A2A link).

Note that, according to the general description of the p-hub median problem, the only locations that are searched for placing the hubs are the locations of the users themselves. In our case, this means that every UAV will be placed right above a distinct user on the ground. Consequently, because all of the UAVs are located at the same altitude h, the total cost introduced by the corresponding p A2G links to users right below the UAVs are constant across all possible combination of UAV placements. For this reason, we do not need to take those costs into account. Finally, we can treat the optimization of UAV placement as a p-hub median problem after appropriate modifications to the original model presented in Equation (1), as follows

$$\text{Minimize:} \quad \sum_{i,j,k,l \in N} T_{ik} X_{ik} + T_{kl} X_{ik} X_{jl} + T_{jl} X_{jl} \qquad (9a)$$

$$\text{Subject to:} \quad \sum_{k=1}^{n} X_{kk} = p, \qquad (9b)$$

$$\sum_{k=1}^{n} X_{ik} = 1, \forall i \in N \qquad (9c)$$

$$X_{ik} \leq X_{kk} \quad \forall i, k \in N \qquad (9d)$$

$$X_{ik} \in \{0,1\} \quad \forall i, k \in N \qquad (9e)$$

Figure 1 depicts the general network scenario of our problem. The full red lines indicate the links between UAVs, while the dashed blue lines show the links between ground users and UAVs. It also displays the key variables used in the formulation of the problem, such as the altitude h of UAVs, the LOS distances between users and UAVs (e.g., d_{ij}), and Euclidean distances between users and UAVs' projections on the ground (e.g., r_{ij}). Figure 1 shows an example where user i can communicate with user j by using the three-hop path that contains UAV k (with link cost T_{ik}), UAV l (with link cost T_{kl}), and user j (with link cost T_{jl}).

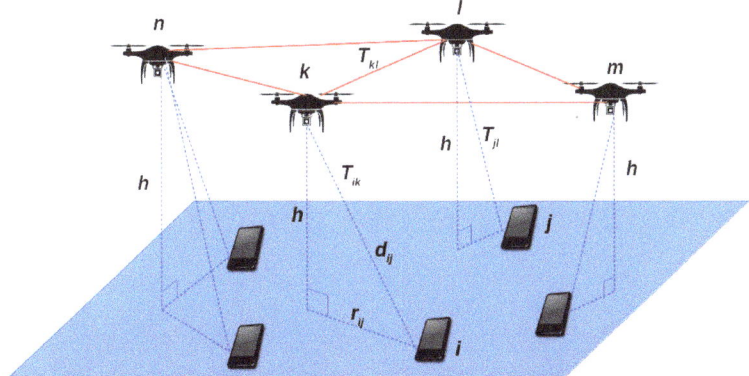

Figure 1. Illustration of a communication between users through user-UAV and UAV-UAV links.

The quadratic integer linear program that is posed by Equation (9a)–(9e) can be linearized and solved by well-known optimization tools, e.g., CPLEX's branch-and-cut optimizer. Nevertheless, as discussed in Section 3.1, the problem may become intractable due to the excessive number of variables and constraints, thus, in the following, we also propose a hybrid optimization methodology integrating a biased randomized (BR) technique with the popular Iterated Local Search (ILS) algorithm, which provides further improvements for the execution time and problem size.

4. The Biased Randomized and Iterated Local Search (BR-ILS) Algorithm

The metaheuristic methodology integrates a Biased Randomized (BR) technique and the Iterated Local Search (ILS) method. The interest of applying such a hybrid strategy is due to the capacity that these techniques have for dealing with different real-world applications. It has been observed that population-based metaheuristics are predominant over single-solution ones when designing communication networks [31]. However, single-solution metaheuristics might offer some advantages over populational approaches. In particular, the ILS metaheuristic employs less parameters and might be easier to implement. By including BR within the ILS, some random choices are included, so that different outcomes at each execution of the metaheuristic are generated. Moreover, the uncapacitated single allocation p-hub median problem is a well-known NP-hard problem. Once the set of hubs is found, the sub-problem of optimal allocation of non-hub nodes to hubs is also NP-hard for $p \geq 3$ [32]. Thus, the application of a hybrid methodology seems to be an appropriate choice.

Even though exact optimization methods provide an assured convergence to the optimal solution, the computational complexity with respect to the problem size may cause severe limitations. Thus, for larger instances, an attractive possibility is the adoption of metaheuristic algorithms, which trade optimality for runtime. These methods allow the resolution of large-scale instances of a specific problem by providing satisfactory solutions in a reasonable execution time.

The ILS, which is a single solution-based method based on the Hill Climbing algorithm [33], explores a sequence of solutions that were created as perturbations of a promising candidate solution. The method finds a solution, known as current solution, and goes to a better solution by exploring the search space in steps within its neighborhood. This better solution is then used as the current solution in the next iteration. The process is repeated until a stop condition is fulfilled. In the ILS approach, the perturbations are applied to the current solution to generate neighboring solutions.

A key point of our proposed methodology is the application of BR during the iterative construction of possible solutions. In this regard, every time that the algorithm constructs a solution, the eligible elements of a feasible solution are ranked according to some criteria, and then chosen according to a skewed probability function biased towards the most promising elements. Among the candidate distributions that are to be considered are the geometric distribution and triangular descendent, among others. However, we pick the geometric distribution, because it only has one parameter (β), which is an attractive choice to be applied in our approach. It assigns higher selection probabilities to more promising solution elements instead of relying, for example, on a restricted candidate list, as some frameworks do [34,35]. This allows us to take advantage of BR features to improve the search space generated by the ILS and, thus, to complement the search [36]. The motivation for implementing hybrid algorithms is usually to obtain better performance approaches that take advantage of the properties of each individual strategy [37]. Algorithm 1 summarizes the logic behind the integration of BR into ILS; hence, named BR-ILS.

The procedure starts by generating an initial solution. The input parameters to the algorithm are: (*i*) the number of users n and the number of UAVs p; (*ii*) the stopping criterion, in our case, it is based on a time limit *maxTime*; (*iii*) the percentage *per* of UAVs of the current solution to be changed during the perturbation stage; (*iv*) the (x, y) coordinates of users *coords*; (*v*) the capacity between users *capacity*; and, (*vi*) the parameter β for the geometric distribution function.

Algorithm 1 General Biased Randomized-Iterated Local Search (BR-ILS) Framework.

Require: $n, p, maxTime, per, coords, capacity, \beta$
Ensure: currentSolution ← generateSolution($n, p, coords, capacity, \beta$) ▷ BR phase
1: bestSolution ← currentSolution
2: credit ← 0
3: **while** stopping criteria is not met **do** ▷ ILS phase
4:     newSolution ← perturbate(currentSolution, per)
5:     proSolution ← localSearch(newSolution)
6:     delta ← cost(currentSolution) - cost(proSolution)
7:     **if** delta ≥ 0 **then**
8:         credit ← delta
9:         currentSolution ← proSolution
10:         **if** cost(proSolution) < cost(bestSolution) **then**
11:             bestSolution ← proSolution
12:         **end if**
13:     **else if** -delta $\leq$ credit **then**
14:         credit ← 0
15:         currentSolution ← proSolution
16:     **end if**
17: **end while**
18: **return** bestSolution

Firstly, the given number p of UAVs among the positioned users are randomly chosen, using a uniform probability distribution. Let k be a candidate location for an UAV and that any user i could be assigned to k. Thus, all of the data transmitted from user i to user j (and vice-versa) has to be sent through UAV k. Accordingly, the inverse of the capacity is computed, i.e., $T_{ik} = 1/C_{ik}$. Moreover, if user j is assigned to an UAV l, then the inverse of the capacity between these UAVs, T_{kl}, is also computed. In order to evaluate the location k as a potential placement of an UAV, we calculate T_{ik} for every positioned user i in the graph, leading to a matrix whose entries are the elements T_{ik}. Subsequently, for each user in the graph, we add the previously selected UAVs in a list that is sorted according to T_{ik}. Subsequently, the BR technique is applied. In order to better illustrate how the BR works, let us compare it to the greedy randomized adaptive search procedure (GRASP) [38]. In such approach, the best element to be chosen at each stage is put into a restricted candidate list, and the element to be included in the solution is randomly selected using a uniform distribution. Contrary to GRASP, when applying BR, all of the elements are eligible to be selected at each step in the construction of a solution. Thus, at each iteration, the possible UAV candidates are taken into account.

Once the initial solution has been generated, the ILS main loop starts. Inside the loop, the current solution is perturbed in order to improve the users' allocations obtained so far, thus generating a new solution. The perturbation occurs by removing a percentage per of the selected UAVs from the current solution. Once a percentage of the UAVs has been removed, the removed ones are replaced by newly selected UAVs; thus, the solution is reconstructed in order to generate a promising solution during this stage. In order to do that, we generate a new assignment of users to UAVs searching into the neighborhood of the current solution.

Subsequently, a local search process is carried out. By following the steps in the local search procedure, the solution approaches the closest local optima by using a neighborhood search scheme. The local search tries to improve the solution at each iteration. Thus, the procedure tries to alternate the selected UAV k with one of the remaining UAVs in the new solution at hands. Once the promising solution is generated, the cost of the solution containing the new UAV configuration is compared to the solution that contains the original UAV. Moreover, the new configuration is chosen following a credit-based system that allows for accepting a new solution, even if this offers a risk, in comparison to the solution at hands. Here, the credit is calculated as the value of the improvement obtained. Thus, the credit value can be seen as an acceptance criterion. If the promising solution improves the current solution, then the current solution is updated. Subsequently, if the promising solution also improves the best solution found so far, it is updated as well. Notice that, in this step, the total (sum) link capacity is calculated, which takes into account the links from the n users allocated to the p UAVs and the links between UAVs. At any time, the best solution found is updated and saved. The loop is executed until the time-based stopping criterion is reached. In the end, the algorithm returns the best solution. All in all, the BR-ILS is a simple and easy-to-implement procedure. As for the complexity of BR-ILS, the time spent is bounded by the predefined time limit $maxTime$. Within the while loop (line 3 of Algorithm 1), the perturbate function consists in removing a random set of UAVs and selecting another random set, this can be executed in $\mathcal{O}(n \cdot p \log p)$. The localSearch function consists in changing the assigned UAV of each user and has a complexity of $\mathcal{O}(n \cdot p)$. Therefore, each iteration of the while loop has a total complexity of $\mathcal{O}(n \cdot p \log p)$.

5. Experimental Study

The proposed approach for the optimization aims at the efficient positioning of the UAVs in order to obtain the best possible coverage while maximizing link capacity. The proposed model was numerically analyzed for its efficiency on the basis of the parameters and configurations that are presented in this section. Test problems of size $n = \{10, 20, 30, 50, 100, 200\}$ and $p = \{3, 10\}$ were generated and solved. Each instance was generated spreading the nodes in a 5 km × 5 km area following a Uniform spatial distribution. For each problem, the capacity was calculated according to Equation (6) and the parameters for simulations are presented in Table 1. A complete list with the generated instances can be downloaded from github.com/Stephdnie/p-UAV-instances. The proposed BR-ILS algorithm was implemented while using Java® 7SE applications. The vast amount of tools available in the standard API of Java and its objected-orientation made the development process easy. A standard personal computer was used to perform all tests, an Intel® Core® i7-3520M CPU @ 2.90 GHz and 12 GB RAM running the Windows® 10 operating system.

Table 1. Simulation Parameters.

Parameters	Description
Carrier frequency f_c	2 GHz
UAVs altitude h	2000 m
Transmission gain G_t	0 dBi
Reception gain G_r	0 dBi
Thermal noise power σ	−90 dBm
UAV transmission power	20 dBm
User transmission power	20 dBm
Channel bandwidth	20 MHz

During the implementation process of the BR-ILS, some of the details that required attention were found, especially: (i) The meticulous design of the different classes so that a convenient level of coupling and cohesion was reached; (ii) The quality of the Random Number Generator to perform random choices during the exploration of the space, which impacts directly the performance of our algorithm. We used the LFSR113 from the SSJ library created by L'ecuyer et al. [39] in order to overcome this situation. This generator provides a period of 2^{113}, compared to the period 2^{48} of the generator provided by the standard Java library; and (iii) The level of precision used to store and operate with numerical values was key to reach the fastness of the proposed BR-ILS. The necessary algorithm parameters to complete the tests were specified, as follows: the maximum time during the ILS block was set to $maxTime = 900$ s; the Geometric distribution parameter β and the percentage per were randomly chosen in the interval $(0.1, 0.3)$.

In the following, a complete analysis of the results is presented and, for that purpose, a test-bench that runs the BR-ILS algorithm was set for running a total of ten times, collecting information regarding the performance of the algorithm, each of them running with a different simulation seed. To assess the performance obtained, a gap is defined as the percentage difference between the (potentially) optimal solution, previously found by CPLEX, and the one found by the algorithm. In addition, run-time information is used to compare the efficiency of both methods.

Table 2 shows a comparison of the results obtained by using both our proposed BR-ILS algorithm and the branch-and-cut algorithm, whose implementation is provided by the optimization software ILOG CPLEX Version 12.10.0 by IBM®. This software tool was chosen due to its wide adoption among operations research community and its reliability [40]. The optimizer automatically determines smart settings for a wide range of algorithm parameters, usually resulting in optimal linear programming solution performance. However, due to restrictions that are imposed by the limited memory and CPU clock, it was necessary to manually turn off the aggregator, clique generator, the heuristic, and to set the optimizer time limit to CPXPARAM_TimeLimit = 10,000 s. With these settings, CPLEX is capable of finding optimal solutions as long as a sufficiently large timeframe is provided; otherwise, it will provide a near-optimal solution. Finally, since the branch-and-cut method is deterministic, it is executed only once per instance.

The table is organized as follows: (i) The first three columns show the size of the instances classified as Small and Large, the number of users represented with n, and the number p of UAVs to be selected; (ii) The next two columns, denoted by Cost (1) and Time give the solution found by the solver CPLEX, and the time it took to find it; (iii) The last three columns, denoted by Cost (2), SD, Time, and Gap, give the average cost of the found solutions, the standard deviation, the average run-time, and the corresponding percentage deviation (gap) with respect to the Cost (1) when applying our proposed BR-ILS metaheuristic for the aforementioned sets of generated instances. The elapsed times are shown in seconds.

Table 2. Comparison of the results that were obtained with CPLEX and BR-ILS.

Instance			CPLEX		BR-ILS			
	n	p	Cost (1)	Time (s)	Cost (2)	SD	Time (s)	Gap %
Small	10	3	9.4373	180.50	9.4373	0.00	0.12	0.00
	20		33.6638	907.34	33.6638	0.00	0.27	0.00
	30		70.4836	7204.41	70.4836	0.00	0.45	0.00
	40		134.3173	7202.50	120.0516	0.00	0.70	−10.72
	50		–	–	179.2856	0.00	0.81	–
Large	100	10	–	–	773.9002	0.00	116.09	–
	200		–	–	2847.7467	0.34	476.30	–

Notice that, for instances that are larger than 50 users and three UAVs, the results obtained by CPLEX were not included, because the solver was not able to find a feasible solution, due to time and memory requirements. In particular, for the instance with 40 users and 3 UAVs, CPLEX finds a worse solution than the one found by BR-ILS, in a much longer time. This situation indicates that the 10,000 s timeframe allowed CPLEX to find a feasible solution, although non-optimal. Furthermore, because BR-ILS is a non-deterministic metaheuristic, it is important to note that the aforementioned results are stable, i.e., present low variability. This is indicated by the zero SD of the Cost observed for all instances, except for the $n = 200$, $p = 10$ case which, however, also presents a relatively low level of variation, i.e., just 0.34 over an average cost of 2847.7467. Thus, the results indicate a good level of stability for the method, obtaining almost identical solutions for all instances and runs. All in all, the results that are shown in Table 2 can be considered to be satisfactory, because, for most of the instances, the standard deviation as well as the computation times indicate the capacity of the BR-ILS algorithm to obtain good quality solutions in a few seconds.

For illustration purposes, Figure 2 displays the configuration of the network when the algorithm is applied for solving the instance with $n = 20$ and $p = 3$. Figure 2a displays the distribution of users in the area without allocating the UAVs. Figure 2b illustrates the positions of users selected as UAVs, as well as the assignments that were provided by the solution. Once our methodology is applied, the algorithm is able to find the best placement of UAVs, and the set of users assigned to the selected UAVs. The UAVs are represented with a squared symbol.

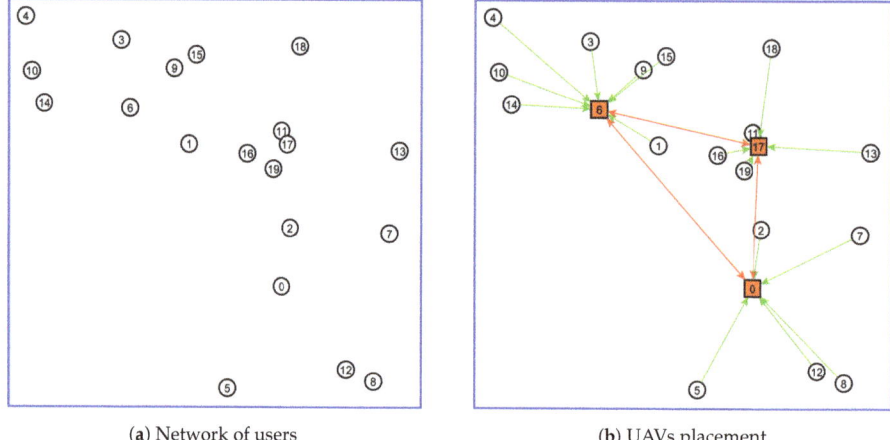

(a) Network of users (b) UAVs placement

Figure 2. Network with 20 users and the resulting optimal placement of 3 UAVs.

Figure 3 graphically summarizes the total inverse link capacity that was obtained when the UAVs are placed following a Naive heuristic versus the total inverse link capacity obtained when the BR-ILS algorithm is applied. The Naive heuristic consists of dividing the area in equal parts depending on the number of UAVs. In particular, for three UAVs, the area is divided into three equal subareas. Following, the centroid of each subarea is found and the UAVs are placed as close as possible to the centroid. Finally, the users in each subarea are assigned to the selected UAVs. Notice the improvement that is obtained in terms of the total cost with the adoption of the proposed methodology. On average, the total link capacity (or, similarly, the total cost) is improved by 12.24% when the UAVs are placed by using BR-ILS.

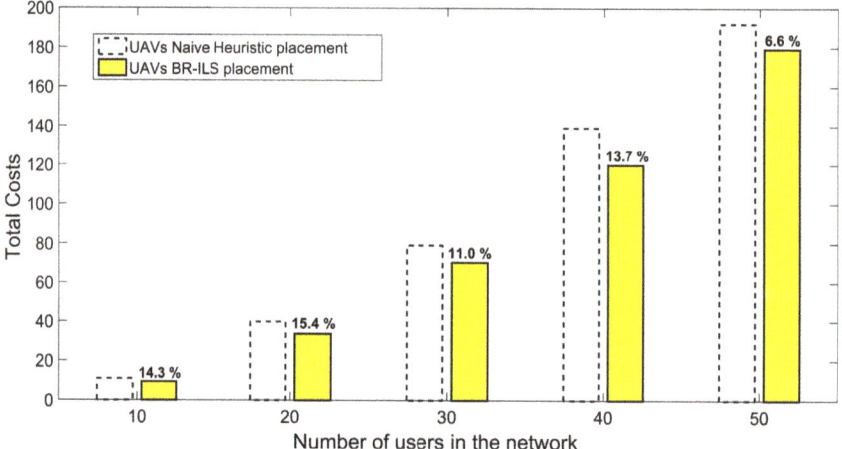

Figure 3. Comparison between the total cost (inverse link capacity) obtained with a Naive heuristic versus the total cost resulting from the application of the proposed BR-ILS algorithm.

6. Conclusions

In this paper, we have treated the UAV placement problem to deploy a wireless infrastructure for communications in the context of disaster relief, rescue operations, and providing user connectivity in remote or hostile environments. The UAVs serve as aerial relays to connect users on the ground, and we seek to maximize the total link capacity of the aerial communication infrastructure. The problem is recognized as a typical p-hub median problem, with a mathematical formulation developed in order to consider the air-to-ground and air-to-air propagation model.

The mixed integer linear programming formulation is optimized via the classical CPLEX branch-and-cut algorithm and via a hybrid metaheuristic, the BR-ILS. The latter is proposed in order to obtain reduced computational cost in association with optimal or close-to optimal solutions. The experimental results show that BR-ILS largely outperforms CPLEX solver for small and large-sized instances, in terms of execution time, while achieving zero gap for the instances whose optimal solution could be obtained by CPLEX. Moreover, when compared to a naive heuristic allocation strategy, the BR-ILS algorithm is able to deliver an average improvement of about 12% for the total cost when different numbers of users are uniformly scattered on the ground. Finally, it is worth mentioning that the BR-ILS algorithm is relatively simple: it has been applied to the tested instances without requiring any special fine-tuning or set-up process, which makes it an appealing tool to support the solution of the UAV placement problem.

Future work involves extending the problem formulation and experimental analysis to more diverse scenarios and parameters, considering flows of data packets between users and other wireless network setups. In fact, the formulation of the p-hub median problem allows for its extension to consider individual flows of packets between users, which is a quite useful feature of this optimization problem. This means that one can consider the actual traffic load that is imposed on each end-to-end connection established between two any users on the ground. However, to treat this problem, one needs to carefully address the impact of channel errors on packet transmissions within each link searched by the algorithm. Moreover, depending on the application scenario, the characteristics and statistics of the packet flows need to be carefully addressed, so they can be properly incorporated into the proposed framework. Furthermore, the adaptation of BR-ILS to other versions of the p-hub median problem is possible. One of the interesting variants of this problem is the capacitated version [41] and, therefore, another orientation for future research could be to consider a fixed link capacity for each UAV. Under these conditions, the mathematical model may include the capacity restrictions.

Author Contributions: Conceptualization, S.A.F., M.M.C. and D.G.S.; methodology, S.A.F., M.M.C. and D.G.S.; software, S.A.F.; validation, S.A.F.; formal analysis, S.A.F.; investigation, S.A.F.; resources, S.A.F. and D.G.S.; data curation, S.A.F.; writing—original draft preparation, S.A.F., M.M.C. and D.G.S.; writing—review and editing, S.A.F., M.M.C. and D.G.S.; visualization, S.A.F.; supervision, S.A.F., M.M.C. and D.G.S. All authors have read and agreed to the published version of the manuscript.

Funding: This study was financed in part by the Coordenação de Aperfeiçoamento de Pessoal de Nível Superior—Brasil (CAPES)—Finance Code 001.

Conflicts of Interest: The authors declare no conflict of interest.

References

1. Zeng, Y.; Zhang, R.; Lim, T.J. Wireless communications with unmanned aerial vehicles: Opportunities and challenges. *IEEE Commun. Mag.* **2016**, *54*, 36–42. [CrossRef]
2. Bekmezci, I.; Sahingoz, O.K.; Temel, Ş. Flying ad-hoc networks (FANETs): A survey. *Ad Hoc Netw.* **2013**, *11*, 1254–1270. [CrossRef]
3. Barka, E.; Kerrache, C.A.; Lagraa, N.; Lakas, A.; Calafate, C.T.; Cano, J.C. UNION: A trust model distinguishing intentional and UNIntentional misbehavior in inter-UAV communicatiON. *J. Adv. Transp.* **2018**, *2018*, 7475357. [CrossRef]

4. Fang, W.; Zhang, W.; Chen, W.; Gao, W.; Jia, G. IONSS: Indirect Observation Node Selection Scheme in Trust Management for UAV Network. In Proceedings of the IEEE Globecom Workshops, Waikoloa, HI, USA, 9–13 December 2019; pp. 1–6.
5. Zeng, Y.; Wu, Q.; Zhang, R. Accessing from the Sky: A Tutorial on UAV Communications for 5G and Beyond. *Proc. IEEE* **2019**, *107*, 2327–2375. [CrossRef]
6. Alzenad, M.; El-Keyi, A.; Lagum, F.; Yanikomeroglu, H. 3-D placement of an unmanned aerial vehicle base station (UAV-BS) for energy-efficient maximal coverage. *IEEE Wirel. Commun. Lett.* **2017**, *6*, 434–437. [CrossRef]
7. Alzenad, M.; El-Keyi, A.; Yanikomeroglu, H. 3-D placement of an unmanned aerial vehicle base station for maximum coverage of users with different QoS requirements. *IEEE Wirel. Commun. Lett.* **2018**, *7*, 38–41. [CrossRef]
8. Kalantari, E.; Yanikomeroglu, H.; Yongacoglu, A. On the Number and 3D Placement of Drone Base Stations in Wireless Cellular Networks. In Proceedings of the IEEE 84th Vehicular Technology Conference (VTC-Fall), Montreal, QC, Canada, 18–21 September 2016; pp. 1–6.
9. Lyu, J.; Zeng, Y.; Zhang, R.; Lim, T.J. Placement Optimization of UAV-Mounted Mobile Base Stations. *IEEE Commun. Lett.* **2017**, *21*, 604–607. [CrossRef]
10. Chen, J.; Gesbert, D. Optimal positioning of flying relays for wireless networks: A LOS map approach. In Proceedings of the IEEE International Conference on Communications (ICC), Paris, France, 21–25 May 2017; pp. 1–6.
11. He, H.; Zhang, S.; Zeng, Y.; Zhang, R. Joint altitude and beamwidth optimization for UAV-enabled multiuser communications. *IEEE Commun. Lett.* **2018**, *22*, 344–347. [CrossRef]
12. Marinho, M.A.; Ferreira, R.S.J.; da Costa, J.P.C.; de Freitas, E.P.; Antreich, F.; Liu, K.; So, H.C.; Rafael, T.; Zelenovsky, R. Antenna array based positioning scheme for unmanned aerial vehicles. In Proceedings of the 17th International ITG Workshop on Smart Antennas (WSA 2013), Stuttgart, Germany, 13–14 March 2013; pp. 1–6.
13. Valavanis, K.P.; Vachtsevanos, G.J. *Handbook of Unmanned Aerial Vehicles*; Springer: Berlin/Heidelberg, Germany, 2015.
14. Merwaday, A.; Guvenc, I. UAV assisted heterogeneous networks for public safety communications. In Proceedings of the 2015 IEEE wireless communications and networking conference workshops (WCNCW), New Orleans, LA, USA, 9–12 March 2015; pp. 329–334.
15. Liu, Y.; Qin, Z.; Cai, Y.; Gao, Y.; Li, G.Y.; Nallanathan, A. UAV communications based on non-orthogonal multiple access. *IEEE Wirel. Commun.* **2019**, *26*, 52–57. [CrossRef]
16. Sharma, V.; Sabatini, R.; Ramasamy, S. UAVs assisted delay optimization in heterogeneous wireless networks. *IEEE Commun. Lett.* **2016**, *20*, 2526–2529. [CrossRef]
17. Sharma, V.; Srinivasan, K.; Chao, H.C.; Hua, K.L.; Cheng, W.H. Intelligent deployment of UAVs in 5G heterogeneous communication environment for improved coverage. *J. Netw. Comput. Appl.* **2017**, *85*, 94–105. [CrossRef]
18. Ur Rahman, S.; Kim, G.H.; Cho, Y.Z.; Khan, A. Deployment of an SDN-based UAV network: Controller placement and tradeoff between control overhead and delay. In Proceedings of the 2017 International Conference on Information and Communication Technology Convergence (ICTC), Jeju, Korea, 18–20 October 2017; pp. 1290–1292.
19. Wang, H.; Wang, W.; Huang, J.; Huo, D.; Xu, Y. Modeling multiple unmanned aerial vehicles placement problem in ad hoc network via quadratic unconstrained binary optimization. In Proceedings of the 2013 International Conference on Unmanned Aircraft Systems (ICUAS), Atlanta, GA, USA, 28-31 May 2013; pp. 926–932.
20. Rosário, D.; Arnaldo Filho, J.; Rosário, D.; Santosy, A.; Gerla, M. A relay placement mechanism based on UAV mobility for satisfactory video transmissions. In Proceedings of the 2017 16th Annual Mediterranean Ad Hoc Networking Workshop (Med-Hoc-Net), Budva, Montenegro, 28–30 June 2017; pp. 1–8.
21. Rosário, D.; Zhao, Z.; Silva, C.; Cerqueira, E.; Braun, T. An OMNET++ framework to evaluate video transmission in mobile wireless multimedia sensor networks. In Proceedings of the 6th International ICST Conference on Simulation Tools and Techniques, Cannes France, March, 6–8 March 2013; ICST (Institute for Computer Sciences, Social-Informatics and Telecommunications Engineering): Brussels, Belgium, 2013; pp. 277–284.

22. Xu, X.; Duan, L.; Li, M. UAV placement games for optimal wireless service provision. In Proceedings of the WiOpt 2018, Shanghai, China, 7–11 May 2018; pp. 1–8.
23. Kim, D.Y.; Lee, J.W. Joint Mission Assignment and Location Management for UAVs in Mission-critical Flying Ad Hoc Networks. In Proceedings of the 2018 International Conference on Information and Communication Technology Convergence (ICTC), Jeju, Korea, 17–19 October 2018; pp. 323–328.
24. Rautu, D.; Dhaou, R.; Chaput, E. Initial placement optimization for multi-channel UAV networks. In Proceedings of the International Conference on Ad-Hoc Networks and Wireless, Luxembourg, 1–3 October 2019; pp. 452–466.
25. Wzorek, M.; Berger, C.; Doherty, P. Router Node Placement in Wireless Mesh Networks for Emergency Rescue Scenarios. In Proceedings of the Pacific Rim International Conference on Artificial Intelligence, Cuvu, Fiji, 26–30 August 2019; pp. 496–509.
26. Ernst, A.T.; Krishnamoorthy, M. Exact and heuristic algorithms for the uncapacitated multiple allocation p-hub median problem. *Eur. J. Oper. Res.* **1998**, *104*, 100–112. [CrossRef]
27. O'kelly, M.E. A quadratic integer program for the location of interacting hub facilities. *Eur. J. Oper. Res.* **1987**, *32*, 393–404. [CrossRef]
28. Ernst, A.T.; Krishnamoorthy, M. Efficient algorithms for the uncapacitated single allocation p-hub median problem. *Locat. Sci.* **1996**, *4*, 139–154. [CrossRef]
29. Ebery, J. Solving large single allocation p-hub problems with two or three hubs. *Eur. J. Oper. Res.* **2001**, *128*, 447–458. [CrossRef]
30. Friis, H.T. A note on a simple transmission formula. *Proc. IRE* **1946**, *34*, 254–256. [CrossRef]
31. Fernandez, S.A.; Juan, A.A.; de Armas Adrián, J.; e Silva, D.G.; Terrén, D.R. Metaheuristics in Telecommunication Systems: Network Design, Routing, and Allocation Problems. *IEEE Syst. J.* **2018**, *12*, 3948–3957. [CrossRef]
32. Love, R.F.; Morris, J.G.; Wesolowsky, G.O. *Facilities Location*; Appleton & Lange: New York, NY, USA, 1988.
33. Langley, P.; Gennari, J.H.; Iba, W. Hill-climbing theories of learning. In Proceedings of the Fourth International Workshop on Machine Learning, Irvine, CA, USA, 22–25 June 1987; pp. 312–323.
34. Festa, P.; Resende, M.G. An annotated bibliography of GRASP—Part I: Algorithms. *Int. Trans. Oper. Res.* **2009**, *16*, 1–24. [CrossRef]
35. Festa, P.; Resende, M.G. An annotated bibliography of GRASP—Part II: Applications. *Int. Trans. Oper. Res.* **2009**, *16*, 131–172. [CrossRef]
36. Alvarez Fernandez, S. A Metaheuristic and Simheuristic Approach for the *p*-Hub Median Problem from a Telecommunication Perspective. Ph.D. Thesis, University of Brasília, Brasília, Brazil, 2018.
37. Raidl, G.R. A unified view on hybrid metaheuristics. In *Hybrid Metaheuristics*; Springer: Berlin/Heidelberg, Germany, 2006; Volume 4030, pp. 1–12.
38. Feo, T.A.; Resende, M.G. Greedy randomized adaptive search procedures. *J. Glob. Optim.* **1995**, *6*, 109–133. [CrossRef]
39. L'ecuyer, P.; Simard, R.; Chen, E.J.; Kelton, W.D. An object-oriented random-number package with many long streams and substreams. *Oper. Res.* **2002**, *50*, 1073–1075. [CrossRef]
40. IBM. IBM ILOG CPLEX Optimization Studio. 2020. Available online: https://www.ibm.com/products/ilog-cplex-optimization-studio/details (accessed on 27 October 2012).
41. Ernst, A.T.; Krishnamoorthy, M. Solution algorithms for the capacitated single allocation hub location problem. *Ann. Oper. Res.* **1999**, *86*, 141–159. [CrossRef]

Publisher's Note: MDPI stays neutral with regard to jurisdictional claims in published maps and institutional affiliations.

© 2020 by the authors. Licensee MDPI, Basel, Switzerland. This article is an open access article distributed under the terms and conditions of the Creative Commons Attribution (CC BY) license (http://creativecommons.org/licenses/by/4.0/).

Article

A Clustering Routing Algorithm Based on Improved Ant Colony Optimization Algorithms for Underwater Wireless Sensor Networks

Xingxing Xiao [1,2,3] **and Haining Huang** [1,2,3,*]

1. Institute of Acoustics, Chinese Academy of Sciences, Beijing 100190, China; xiaoxingxing@mail.ioa.ac.cn
2. Key Laboratory of Science and Technology on Advanced Underwater Acoustic Signal Processing, Chinese Academy of Sciences, Beijing 100190, China
3. School of Electronic, Electrical and Communication Engineering, University of Chinese Academy of Sciences, Beijing 100049, China
* Correspondence: hhn@mail.ioa.ac.cn

Received: 15 August 2020; Accepted: 30 September 2020; Published: 1 October 2020

Abstract: Because of the complicated underwater environment, the efficiency of data transmission from underwater sensor nodes to a sink node (SN) is faced with great challenges. Aiming at the problem of energy consumption in underwater wireless sensor networks (UWSNs), this paper proposes an energy-efficient clustering routing algorithm based on an improved ant colony optimization (ACO) algorithm. In clustering routing algorithms, the network is divided into many clusters, and each cluster consists of one cluster head node (CHN) and several cluster member nodes (CMNs). This paper optimizes the CHN selection based on the residual energy of nodes and the distance factor. The selected CHN gathers data sent by the CMNs and transmits them to the sink node by multiple hops. Optimal multi-hop paths from the CHNs to the SN are found by an improved ACO algorithm. This paper presents the ACO algorithm through the improvement of the heuristic information, the evaporation parameter for the pheromone update mechanism, and the ant searching scope. Simulation results indicate the high effectiveness and efficiency of the proposed algorithm in reducing the energy consumption, prolonging the network lifetime, and decreasing the packet loss ratio.

Keywords: underwater wireless sensor networks; ant colony optimization algorithms; clustering routing algorithms; energy efficiency; network lifetime

1. Introduction

Nowadays, underwater wireless sensor networks (UWSNs) have aroused widespread interest with the exploration and utilization of marine resources [1,2]. UWSNs are composed of numerous underwater acoustic sensor nodes deployed in underwater monitoring areas, which perform functions such as navigation, surveillance, resource exploration, intrusion detection, and data collection [3]. However, the underwater sensor nodes are small devices with limited energy and they are difficult to replace, which makes energy efficiency a major concern [4,5]. Moreover, UWSNs have disadvantages such as high propagation delay, low bandwidth, and high error rate [6]. Therefore, designing an energy-efficient routing algorithm for data transmission in a complex underwater environment is extremely important for UWSNs [7]. There exist many conventional routing algorithms in terrestrial wireless sensor networks (TWSNs), but they are usually infeasible in UWSNs [8]. The reasons are as follows. Firstly, TWSNs employ radio signals to transmit data, but UWSNs use acoustic signals for data transmission because radio signals attenuate quickly underwater [9]. Secondly, TWSNs usually employ a 2D network model, whereas UWSNs adopt a 3D network model, which is a great challenge to researchers. Thirdly, the replacement of sensor nodes is more difficult in UWSNs than in TWSNs.

In conserving energy, multi-hop data transmission in long-distance communication for UWSNs is more effective than single-hop transmission [10]. Additionally, to alleviate the problems of data collision and traffic load balance, it is important to design a reliable network topology [11]. Many studies have shown that the clustering routing algorithm is capable of saving energy, avoiding collisions, and balancing traffic load because it employs the clustering topology and uses a multi-hop mechanism during the inter-cluster data transmission [12,13]. In clustering routing algorithms, the network is divided into many clusters and each cluster consists of one cluster head node (CHN) and several cluster member nodes (CMNs) [14]. When clusters are formed, the CHNs allocate channel resources for CMNs and the CMNs transmit data according to the allocation, which can decrease collisions [15]. After receiving the data from the CMNs in the same cluster, the CHN is responsible for aggregating the data, which can reduce data redundancy and decrease the number of data packets to be sent to the sink node (SN), thereby conserving energy [16]. Meanwhile, the decreased number of data packets helps reduce collisions when the CHNs transmit them to the SN. Additionally, the multi-hop mechanism is used when CHNs send data to the SN, which can save energy compared to the single-hop mechanism. Moreover, the clustering routing algorithm usually employs a CHN rotation mechanism, which avoids the excessive energy consumption of CHNs, balances the energy dissipation, and prolongs the network lifetime [17].

Many studies indicate that clustering routing algorithms are superior in controlling data traffic and reducing data transmission, and are thus capable of saving energy, extending network lifespan, and decreasing the packet loss ratio [18–28]. The low-energy adaptive clustering hierarchy (LEACH) algorithm, the earliest clustering routing algorithm, employs a probabilistic method to select CHNs and does not consider the residual energy of nodes, which causes some low-energy nodes to become CHNs [18]. This goes against the energy balance and the energy efficiency, for these inefficient CHNs may die prematurely. Therefore, researchers proposed improved clustering routing algorithms. Domingo et al. proposed a distributed underwater clustering scheme (DUCS), which considers the residual energy of candidate nodes when selecting CHNs [19]. However, the distance between the candidate CHN and the SN is not considered in the DUCS algorithm. Xu et al. came up with a clustering routing algorithm where the CHN selection is optimized by considering the remaining energy and the positions and the density of nodes [20]. Additionally, the mechanism of data transmission from the CHN to the SN is improved, thereby minimizing the energy consumption and maximizing the network lifetime. Wang et al. presented a clustering routing protocol based on hybrid multiple hops, where the CHN selection based on the remaining energy of nodes is self-organized and the path from CHN to the destination node is obtained by the establishment of a minimum spanning tree [21]. This algorithm can reduce energy consumption and extend the network expectancy, but is designed for TWSNs instead of UWSNs. Wan et al. designed an adaptive clustering underwater network (ACUN) algorithm, which considers the residual energy of nodes and the energy loss of paths to select CHNs [22]. It also considers the node energy condition to select paths with high energy efficiency. However, the distance factor has not been considered in this literature. Bhattacharjya et al. proposed a cluster-based underwater wireless sensor network (CUWSN) algorithm, which selects CHNs based on the residual energy of nodes and adopts multi-hop transmission to forward data packets to the destination node [23]. The CUWSN can reduce energy consumption and improve the performance of the network, but the distance factor has not been taken into account and the multi-hop paths have not been optimized. In [24], Ayaz et al. did a survey on routing algorithms in UWSNs, which aimed to solve problems such as data transmitting and node deployment, as well as localization. In the survey, the authors analyzed and compared several clustering routing algorithms such as the DUCS [19], the distributed minimum cost clustering protocol (MCCP) [25], temporary cluster-based routing (TCBR) [26], the location-based clustering algorithm for data gathering (LCAD) [27], and the multipath virtual sink architecture [28]. The MCCP was proposed by Pu et al. in [25], which addresses the hotspots near the SN and balances the traffic load. In addition, the MCCP determines the number of CMNs according to the locations of the CHNs and the SN. However, the multi-hop method is not supported in the MCCP and the period of re-clustering is too long. TCBR was presented by Ayaz et al. in [26], where multiple SNs are placed on the water's surface in order to solve the problem that nodes near the SN consume more energy and die prematurely. TCBR can balance the energy dissipation, but it cannot achieve high efficiency in time-critical applications. The LCAD was given by Anupama et al. in [27], where horizontal acoustic communication is employed when CMNs transmit data to CHNs, and autonomous underwater vehicles (AUVs) are used when CHNs send data to the SN. The LCAD can solve the energy hole problem and reduce energy dissipation. However, it relies on the network structure and its effectiveness is affected if the node mobility is considered. The multipath virtual sink architecture was proposed by Seah and Tan in [28], where the aggregation nodes aggregate the data from other nodes in the same cluster, and then transmit the aggregated data to the SNs. The authors assume that these SNs can achieve high-speed communications so that they form a virtual SN. This method can guarantee high reliability, but the duplicate data packets result in redundant transmission, which increases the resource consumption. A pressure routing algorithm for UWSNs was presented by Uichin et al. in [29], which employs anycast routing to send data to the SN according to the pressure levels. Pressure routing can achieve high delivery ratios and low end-to-end delay, but it consumes more energy because of the use of opportunistic routing and the repeated transmission of the copies of same packets. The cluster sleep–wake scheduling algorithm in UWSNs was proposed by Zhang et al. in [30], which shows the rotating temporary control nodes that control the sleep–wake scheduling, thus minimizing the energy dissipation. The energy optimization clustering algorithm (EOCA) was put forward by Yu et al. in [11], where the number of neighboring nodes, the remaining energy of nodes, the motion of nodes, and the distance factor are taken into account. Additionally, the EOCA provides a maximum effective communication range based on the remaining energy of nodes, thereby controlling the energy dissipation for packet delivery. However, the EOCA does not optimize the multi-hop paths for data transmission to the SN.

Greedy algorithms have shown great strength in addressing combinational optimization problems, which make local optimal choices at every step [31,32]. They are effective in finding global optimal solutions in specific circumstances [33], and we take Dijkstra's algorithm and Prim's algorithm as examples [34,35]. Dijkstra's algorithm, which was proposed by Edsger Wybe Dijkstra in 1959, has been widely used to look for the shortest paths between network nodes. It can thus be employed in routing algorithms to find the shortest path to the destination node [36]. Prim's algorithm constructs minimum spanning trees and can usually find the best solutions [37]. Nevertheless, the greedy algorithms are considered short-sighted because they only make the best choice at every step and do not consider the overall condition. That is the reason why they cannot obtain the optimal solution sometimes. Hence, researchers proposed many metaheuristics extending greedy algorithms, which can be applied to a wide range of different problems [38–41]. The greedy randomized adaptive search procedure (GRASP) was presented by Feo et al. in [38], where the present problem can be solved in every iteration. Each iteration has two stages: stage one provides the initial solution and stage two aims to find the improved solution by applying the local search procedure to the solution provided by stage one. The fixed set search (FSS) was proposed by Jovanovic et al. in [39], which adds the learning method to the GRASP and is thus more effective than the GRASP in the solution quality as well as the computational cost. In the work of Arnaout in [40], the worm optimization (WO), on the basis of the worm behaviors, was proposed to solve unrelated parallel machine schedule problems, which can find the optimal solution as well as reduce the makespan. In [41], the particle swarm optimization (PSO) and the fuzzy algorithm are used in a clustering scheme for UWSNs, which can find the optimal number of clusters and select the optimal CHNs, thereby reducing the energy dissipation and prolonging the lifespan of UWSNs.

The ant colony optimization (ACO) algorithm is also a population-based metaheuristic that extends the greedy algorithm, which has been widely used to optimize routing paths [42–44]. The ACO can find optimal paths from source nodes to destination nodes so that the energy consumption can be reduced and the network lifetime can be prolonged. ACO algorithms simulate ant behavior, as ants could usually find the optimal paths to foods [45]. Ants release pheromones on the path that they make. Other ants are more likely to choose the path with higher pheromone concentration, and the following ants will also release pheromones on the path, which increases the pheromone concentration [46]. The higher pheromone concentration will attract more ants, which forms a positive feedback loop. After a period of time, the ant colony will find the shortest path to the food source.

So far, many researchers have applied ACO algorithms to routing algorithms. Agarwal et al. combined ACO algorithms with the LEACH algorithm for prolonging the lifetime of TWSNs, and they validated the effectiveness of the algorithm by simulation experiments [47]. Okdem et al. applied ACO algorithms to routing algorithms by taking into account the hop count and the residual energy of neighbor nodes, which can reduce the energy consumption to a certain extent, but the algorithm can only balance the local energy consumption [48]. Camilo et al. improved the pheromone update process of ACO algorithms when designing routing algorithms, and took into account the total energy of all nodes, thereby improving the energy efficiency of the entire network [49]. Shan proposed a threat cost calculation for submarine path planning based on ACO algorithms [50]. He presented a new cost function that took into account the path length and distance factor, and adopted a coalescing differential evolution mechanism when updating the pheromone so as to settle the local optimum problem. Zhang et al. proposed a clustering algorithm on the basis of the ACO algorithm, which was designed for TWSNs instead of UWSNs. When selecting CHNs, they considered the residual energy of candidate nodes and the distance factor. When looking for routing paths, the authors took into account the path length as well as the node energy, which can balance the network energy consumption [51]. Sun et al. presented a routing protocol based on ACO algorithms for TWSNs, where the remaining energy of nodes, the transmission direction, and the distance between nodes were considered in order to look for ideal routing paths and reduce the energy consumption of the network [52]. Liu proposed an effective transmission strategy using ACO algorithms, which can improve the energy efficiency and prolong the network lifetime. Additionally, the improved ACO algorithm was unlike the traditional one: no heuristic information and just one step for every ant in its whole trip [53]. The literature mentioned above indicate that ACO algorithms could be employed to look for the optimal routing paths in networks. Nevertheless, the problem of clustering routing algorithms in UWSNs has not been resolved, so we need to make some improvements to the existing ACO algorithms and apply them to UWSNs.

To our knowledge, few studies have applied ACO algorithms in UWSNs when designing clustering routing algorithms. It is of great significance to design an energy-efficient routing algorithm that can minimize the energy consumption and ultimately maximize the network lifetime. Therefore, this paper presents a clustering routing algorithm based on an improved ACO algorithm for UWSNs. Firstly, we describe the network model and the energy consumption model that can be used to quantify energy consumption and evaluate the energy efficiency of the proposed algorithm. Secondly, we present an improved ACO algorithm through the improvement of the heuristic information, the evaporation parameter for the pheromone update mechanism, and the ant searching scope. To improve the heuristic information of the traditional ACO algorithm, we consider not only the residual energy but also the distance factor in the proposed heuristic information. Additionally, the proposed adaptive strategy of the evaporation parameter for the pheromone update mechanism helps improve the global search ability and the convergence rate of the algorithm. Thirdly, we design the clustering routing algorithm, which has two main phases in one round: CHN selection phase and data transmission phase. In the first phase, we optimize CHN selection by considering the residual energy of nodes, the distance from the node to the SN and the average distance between the node and the other nodes in the cube. In the second phase, the single-hop method is adopted for the data transmission from CMNs to CHNs, and the multi-hop method is employed when CHNs transmit data to the SN, and the optimal multi-hop paths are found by the improved ACO algorithm. Finally, simulation results show that compared to five other algorithms, the proposed algorithm can effectively reduce the energy consumption of the network, prolong the network lifetime, and decrease the packet loss ratio.

The remainder of the rest of the paper is as follows. The network model and energy consumption model are presented in Section 2. Section 3 proposes the improved ACO algorithm. The proposed clustering routing algorithm is given in Section 4. Simulation results and analyses are provided in Section 5. Section 6 draws the conclusion.

2. Model Assumptions

2.1. Network Model

This paper presents a large-scale 3D network model for UWSNs where the underwater sensor nodes are randomly deployed in an underwater monitoring area. Figure 1 illustrates the network model and the description is as follows:

1. The 3D underwater network is evenly divided into small cubes and each cube is regarded as a cluster.
2. Two types of nodes are considered in the network: the ordinary underwater acoustic sensor nodes and the SN. The underwater acoustic sensor nodes are static after random deployment.
3. The single SN is always the destination node and is located at the center of the surface of the monitoring area, which has a continuous energy supply. However, the energy of the ordinary sensor nodes is restrained and they do not have an energy supply.
4. All nodes (except the SN) have the same initial energy and every node has a unique ID.
5. The locations of the SN and sensor nodes after placement can be obtained by localization algorithms [54], and the distance between two nodes can be calculated.
6. The sending power can be controlled by nodes according to different distances to the receiving nodes.
7. In every small cube, sensor nodes run for CHN. One of them will become the CHN and the others become CMNs. CMNs collect data and send them to the CHN by a single hop. After receiving the data from the CMNs, the CHN processes the data and then transmits them to the SN in one data packet by multiple hops. The relay nodes on multi-hop paths are other CHNs. If some CHNs are near the SN, they can directly forward data to the SN by a single hop.

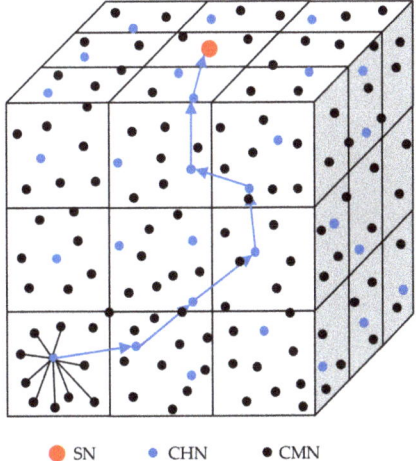

Figure 1. The schematic diagram of the network model.

2.2. Energy Consumption Model

To quantify the energy consumption, this paper refers to the underwater acoustic energy consumption model given in [55]. We assume that the minimum power for one node to receive a data packet is P_0. Then the minimum transmission power needs to be $P_0 A(l)$. $A(l)$ is the attenuation function, which is presented by:

$$A(l) = l^k a^l \tag{1}$$

where l is the distance between transmitter node and receiver node and k is the energy spreading factor (1 for cylindrical, 2 for spherical, 1.5 in general), and

$$a = 10^{\alpha(f)/10} \tag{2}$$

is decided by the absorption coefficient, which is presented by:

$$\alpha(f) = 0.11\frac{f^2}{1+f^2} + 44\frac{f^2}{4100+f^2} + 2.75 \times 10^{-4} f^2 + 0.003 \tag{3}$$

where f is carrier frequency in kHz. Then we can define the energy consumption for sending and receiving:

$$E_t(l) = T_t P_0 A(l) \tag{4}$$

$$E_r = T_r P_0 \tag{5}$$

where $E_t(l)$ and E_r are energy consumption for transmitting and receiving, respectively. T_t and T_r are the time duration for a node to transmit and receive one data packet, respectively. The time duration can be calculated by the data packet length and the data transmission rate.

3. The Improved Strategy of the ACO Algorithm

3.1. Overview of ACO

The ACO algorithm is widely used to find an optimal path between a source node and a destination node. When searching for the destination node, artificial ants deposit a chemical substance called a pheromone on the path that they pass [56]. The pheromone is the medium that ants used to communicate and it guides other ants. Ants are more likely to follow a path with a higher pheromone concentration, and the following ants also release pheromones on the path, which increases the pheromone concentration. The increased pheromone concentration attracts more ants, which forms a positive feedback loop [57]. The pheromone matrix is a two-dimensional matrix used to record the pheromone values on every partial path. We use $\tau_{ij}(t)$ to denote the pheromone concentration between node i and node j at time t. Additionally, t is the iteration counter. Moreover, the pheromone volatilizes with time. After all ants have completed a path search, the pheromone matrix should be updated. The global pheromone update rule is presented as follows:

$$\tau_{ij}(t+1) = (1-\rho)\tau_{ij}(t) + \Delta\tau_{ij}(t) \tag{6}$$

$$\Delta\tau_{ij}(t) = \sum_{k=1}^{q} \Delta\tau_{ij}^k(t) \tag{7}$$

$$\Delta\tau_{ij}^k(t) = \begin{cases} Q/L_k &, (i,j) \in \text{tour byant } k \\ 0 &, \text{otherwise} \end{cases} \tag{8}$$

where ρ ($0 < \rho < 1$) is the evaporation parameter, q is the total number of ants, Q is the total amount of pheromone, and L_k is the total length of the path that the kth ant passes during this time. Nevertheless, a too high pheromone concentration may cause a local optimum of the algorithm and a too low pheromone concentration may not attract other ants. Thus, we employ the method introduced in the max–min ant system (MMAS) to limit the pheromone value [58], which is presented as follows:

$$\tau_{ij}(t+1) = \begin{cases} \tau_{max}, & \tau_{ij}(t+1) > \tau_{max} \\ (1-\rho)\tau_{ij}(t) + \Delta\tau_{ij}(t), & \text{otherwise} \\ \tau_{min}, & \tau_{ij}(t+1) < \tau_{min} \end{cases} \quad (9)$$

where τ_{max} and τ_{min} represent the maximum and the minimum of the pheromone values, respectively. The limitation of the pheromone values could avoid the stagnation of the searching process and improve the global convergence of the algorithm.

In ACO, the transition probability from node i to node j for the kth ant can be given by:

$$p_{ij}^k = \begin{cases} \dfrac{(\tau_{ij}(t))^\alpha (\eta_{ij})^\beta}{\sum_{m \in U_k}(\tau_{im}(t))^\alpha (\eta_{im})^\beta}, & j \in U_k \\ 0, & \text{otherwize} \end{cases} \quad (10)$$

where U_k represents the set of next hop nodes available to the ants, η_{ij} is the heuristic information, α is the pheromone parameter, and β denotes the heuristic information parameter.

Ants transfer to the next hop node according to (10) until they arrive at the destination node. After all q ants have reached the destination node, the pheromone matrix is updated. It is decreased by evaporation, and ρ ranging from 0 to 1 is the evaporation parameter. The evaporation process contributes to avoiding unrestrained accumulation of the pheromone concentration. If one partial path is not selected by ants, its pheromone concentration decreases gradually, which makes ants not choose this bad path over time. The pheromone value is increased if the ants deposit pheromone on the path. The better paths receive more pheromone released by ants, which are more likely to be selected in future. Every pheromone value in the pheromone matrix is updated according to (7), (8), and (9). After the pheromone matrix is updated, the next iteration begins.

3.2. The Improved Evaporation Parameter

Researchers have proposed many methods to update the pheromone values. For example, Jovanovic and Tuba put forward a very efficient pheromone correction procedure based on the concept of suspicion, which avoids the local convergence of the ACO and enhances the overall performance of the ACO [59]. In this paper, we aim at the evaporation parameter ρ and propose an adaptive strategy to influence the update of the pheromone values. The evaporation parameter ρ is important to the ACO algorithm. In the most ACO algorithms, ρ is a fixed value. When the value of ρ is unreasonable, the convergence rate of the algorithm is affected. If the value is too small, the pheromone evaporation speed is too slow, making ants just follow the path with a high pheromone concentration and do not try to look for other potential paths. That means the algorithm can easily fall into the local optimum. If the value is too large, the pheromone volatilizes too fast, which causes the ACO to converge slowly. The adaptive strategy for evaporation parameter ρ is given by:

$$\rho(x) = \dfrac{X}{X+x} \times e^{-bx} \quad (11)$$

where X denotes the total number of iterations, x is the current number of iterations, and b is a constant. At the beginning, the pheromone volatilizes faster, and the pheromone concentration has a weaker guiding effect on the ants, which is helpful for the ants to find other potential paths. As the iterations increase, the value of $\rho(x)$ gradually decreases, and the pheromone evaporation slows down. The positive feedback increases, which makes the ants tend to choose the path with a higher pheromone concentration. At this time, the ants have searched for feasible paths for a long time and the path with a higher pheromone concentration is the better choice. So, the proposed strategy is capable of improving the global search ability and the convergence rate of the algorithm.

3.3. The Heuristic Information

The heuristic information η_{ij} is only related to the distance to the next hop node, which can be calculated by:

$$\eta_{ij} = \frac{1}{d_{ij}} \qquad (12)$$

where d_{ij} denotes the distance between node i and the next hop node j. Nevertheless, in UWSNs, the distance from node j to the SN also has an influence on the network energy consumption. If the next hop node j is closer to the SN, it tends to consume less energy to forward data. In addition, the energy of the next hop node also affects the balance of the energy consumption, which helps to prevent the node with low energy becoming the next hop node. Hence, this paper defines an improved strategy for heuristic information:

$$\eta_{ij} = \frac{1}{\sigma d_{ij} + (1-\sigma)d_{js}} \times \frac{E_{jres}}{E_{ini}} \qquad (13)$$

where σ is a constant ranging from 0 to 1, E_{jres} denotes the residual energy of the next hop node j, E_{ini} indicates the initial energy of node j, and d_{js} represents the distance from node j to the SN. From (13), we can see that the heuristic information is positively related to the residual energy of the next hop node j, and is negatively correlated with the distance between node i and node j and the distance from node j to the SN. It is more likely for node j to become the next hop node if the value of the heuristic information is larger.

3.4. The Proposal of Ant Searching Scope

The searching scope is crucial to the algorithm. Too small a scope may result in a failure to find the next hop node and too large a scope could lead to the slow convergence of the algorithm. To alleviate this problem, this paper presents the searching scope, as shown in Figure 2. R presents the transmission radius of nodes and θ denotes the searching scope. The density of nodes in the network and the transmission radius of nodes are two important factors to the searching scope. A high density of nodes and a large transmission radius only require a small scope. Clearly, if the value of θ is smaller, the transmission direction is closer to the SN. Theoretically, when the value of θ is zero, it is the best transmission direction from node i to the SN. However, in fact, there may not be enough nodes existing in that best transmission direction. If an ant cannot find an appropriate next hop node, the searching scope should be enlarged and θ should be smaller than 90 degrees.

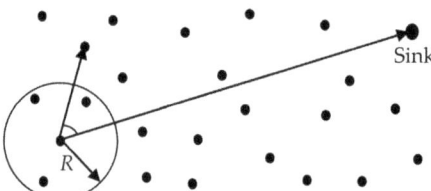

Figure 2. The searching scope.

4. Clustering Routing Algorithm Design

The clustering routing algorithm has two main phases: CHN selection phase and data transmission phase. In the algorithm, the network is divided into cubes, and each cube is seen as a cluster. In every cluster, nodes run for CHN. One of them will be selected as the CHN and the others become CMNs. CMNs collect data and send them to the CHN by a single hop. After receiving the data from the CMNs, the CHN processes the data and then transmits them to the SN in one data packet by multiple hops.

The relay nodes on multi-hop paths are other CHNs and the optimal path to the SN is found by using the improved ACO algorithm.

4.1. Cluster Head Selection Phase

CHNs play a very important role in data transmission. The CHNs are responsible for processing the data received from their CMNs, and then forwarding the processed data to the SN. Many algorithms, such as the LEACH algorithm, generate CHNs in a random selection without considering the residual energy of the nodes. If the residual energy of the selected CHNs is too low, the nodes will die too early, which is bad for energy balance and network efficiency. Therefore, when selecting CHNs, the residual energy of the nodes should be considered. If the residual energy of one node is less than the average energy of the nodes in its cluster, it will not be qualified for the selection. In this paper, we consider not only the residual energy of nodes but also the distance factor to select CHNs. Hence, we propose an index for CHN selection as follows:

$$I_i = \frac{\lambda E_{ires}}{d_{is} d_{avg}} \tag{14}$$

$$d_{avg} = \frac{1}{N-1} \sum_{n=1}^{N-1} d_{in} \tag{15}$$

where λ is a constant, E_{ires} is the residual energy of node i, d_{is} is the distance between node i and the SN, d_{avg} is the average distance between node i and the other nodes in the cube, N is the total number of nodes in the cube, and d_{in} is the distance between node i and node n in the cube. It can be seen from (14) that it is more likely for a node to become a CHN if it has more residual energy, a shorter distance to the SN, and a shorter average distance to the other nodes in the cube.

In each cube, every qualified node calculates its value of I_i and broadcasts the message with its ID and I_i value to other nodes in the cube. Through comparisons, the node with the largest value of I_i will become a CHN. Then the CHN broadcasts the CHN message to the other nodes in the cube. After receiving the CHN message, the nodes reply to the CHN with an acknowledgement message and become CMNs. In addition, all the selected CHNs send message packets to the SN and the packets carry information such as the ID, the location, and the residual energy.

4.2. Data Transmission Phase

The data transmission phase includes intra-cluster data transmission and inter-cluster data transmission. In the intra-cluster data transmission, the CHNs allocate time slots by a time division multiple access (TDMA) scheme for the CMNs to send data packets to their own CHNs by a single hop. After the CMNs transmit the data packets for this round, they turn to sleep mode in order to reduce energy consumption. After receiving the data packets from all the CMNs in the cluster, the CHNs process the data and then transmit them to the SN by using a carrier sense multiple access with collision detection (CSMA/CD) mechanism through multiple hops and the optimal multi-hop paths are found by the improved ACO algorithm. If some CHNs are near the SN, they can directly transmit the data to the SN by a single hop. The process of the improved ACO algorithm is shown in Figure 3 and the steps are given as follows:

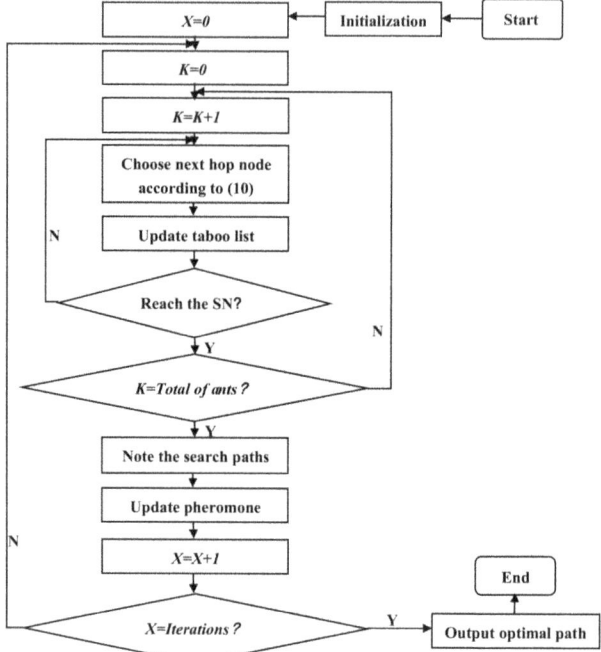

Figure 3. The process of the improved ant colony optimization (ACO) algorithm.

Step 1: To ensure the initial search ability of ants, the initial energy and the initial pheromone concentration of each node are set to be equal. Each node has a unique ID.

Step 2: The source node generates a forward ant at regular intervals. The format of the routing table carried by the forward ant is shown in Table 1. The taboo list indicates the nodes that the ant has visited and these nodes cannot be accessed in future searches.

Table 1. The format of the routing table.

Source Node ID	SN ID	Hop Count	Taboo List	Packet Length	Packet Type

Step 3: The transfer probability to the next hop node is calculated by (10). The ant transfers to the next CHN according to this probability. Then this next hop node is added to the taboo list, and the hop count is increased by one.

Step 4: Step 3 is repeated until the ant reaches the SN. At the same time, the forward ant dies, and the corresponding backward ant is generated. The backward ant carries the routing information of the forward ant and returns to the source node by the path that the forward ant made. The routing information no longer changes as the backward ant returns. When the backward ant reaches the source node, a routing path is established.

Step 5: Steps 2, 3, and 4 are repeated until all ants have completed a path search. By this time, the present iteration ends. Then the search paths of the ants are noted, the taboo list is cleared, and the pheromone is updated according to (9).

Step 6: Steps 2 to 5 are repeated until the preset number of iterations is reached, and the optimal path output is shown.

It is noted that only one CHN finds its optimal path to the SN after Step 6, and the number of CHNs is equal to the number of small cubes in the network. Hence, by changing the IDs of the source nodes and repeating the whole process of the ACO algorithm, the paths from the other CHNs to the SN can be determined. In this paper, the destination node is always the SN and the CHNs that need to send data packets become the source nodes. The relay nodes on multi-hop paths are other CHNs. Furthermore, the search process for the optimal multi-hop routing paths is accomplished in the SN because it has a continuous energy supply. After the CHNs are selected, they send the SN messages with information such as IDs, locations, and residual energy so that the SN can figure out the optimal paths by using the improved ACO and then transmit the routing information to the CHNs.

By the time all the CHNs have sent the data to the SN, one round is over. At this time, if in one cube the residual energy of the CHN is more than half of the average energy of other nodes, the CHN of the next round stays the same, which can save energy and time. Otherwise, a new CHN is selected in the next round. The new selected CHN transmits its information to the SN so that the SN can restart the process of the ACO algorithm and find the optimal path for the new CHN.

5. Simulation Results and Analyses

For the convenience of comparison, the proposed algorithm in this paper is called ant colony optimization clustering routing (ACOCR). Five existing popular algorithms: LEACH [18], DUCS [19], LEACH-ANT [47], CUWSN [23], and EOCA [11] were chosen as the references to validate the proposed algorithm according to the number of surviving nodes, the energy consumption of the network, and the packet loss ratio. MATLAB was used to carry out the simulation where sensor nodes were randomly placed in a 3D area of 5000 m × 5000 m × 1000 m and the coordinate of the SN was (2500, 2500, 0). The network was divided into 64 cubes. The number of sensor nodes ranged from 300 to 500 for different scenarios. The data packet was 1024 bits in length and the data transmission rate was 2048 bps, by which the time duration for a node to transmit and receive data packets could be calculated. The broadcast and other message packets were 64 bits in length. The sound speed was 1500 m/s. As for the energy consumption parameters, the receiving power P_0 was set to 50 µW and the initial energy for every node was 120 J. The frequency f was 10 kHz.

5.1. Comparison and Analysis of the Number of Surviving Nodes

Figure 4 shows the number of surviving nodes versus the number of rounds for the proposed algorithm and reference algorithms when 400 nodes were considered in the network, from which we can see that the number of surviving nodes decreases with the increase in the network rounds no matter which algorithm is used. However, by using the proposed ACOCR, the network always has the largest number of surviving nodes.

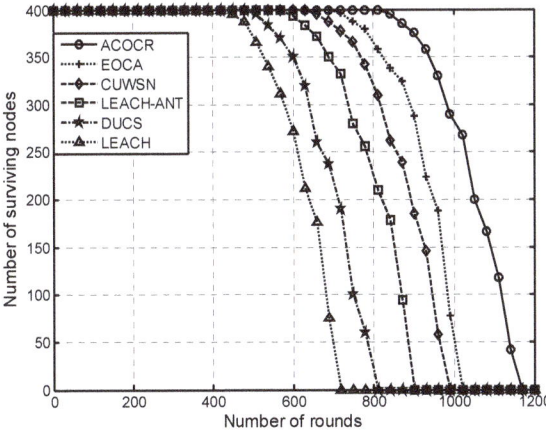

Figure 4. The number of surviving nodes versus the number of rounds for the six algorithms.

In order to further assess the network lifetime, this paper brings in some metrics, such as first node dead (FND), half of the nodes dead (HND), and last node dead (LND). Figure 5 illustrates the number of rounds when FND, HND, and LND arise for the six algorithms, from which we can see that the first node of the ACOCR, EOCA, CUWSN, LEACH-ANT, DUCS, and LEACH dies in about the 806th, 686th, 632th, 569th, 481th, and 423th round, respectively. That indicates that with respect to the FND metric, the efficiency of the proposed ACOCR is 17.5%, 27.5%, 41.7%, 67.6%, and 90.5% higher than that of EOCA, CUWSN, LEACH-ANT, DUCS, and LEACH, respectively. As for the HND and LND, the proposed ACOCR outperforms LEACH by 63.2% and 65.2%, respectively. In conclusion, the proposed ACOCR algorithm has the best performance in prolonging the network lifetime because it adopts the improved CHN selection scheme by comprehensively considering the residual energy of the nodes, the distance between the node and the SN, and the average distance between the node and the other nodes in the cube. The CHN selection is capable of distributing the network load equally and preventing the nodes with low energy from becoming CHNs so as to prevent the premature death of nodes. Additionally, the ACOCR employs the improved ACO to find the optimal paths between CHNs and the SN in order to reduce the energy consumption. The LEACH has the worst performance, as it randomly selects CHNs without considering the residual energy of the nodes, which makes some nodes with insufficient residual energy be selected as CHNs and thus die too early. In addition, it does not consider the multi-hop paths when the CHNs send data packets to the SN. The LEACH-ANT algorithm and the DUCS algorithm outperform the LEACH algorithm. This is because the LEACH-ANT algorithm employs ACO algorithms to look for the next hop node, and the DUCS algorithm selects the CHN according to the residual energy of the node. However, the LEACH-ANT algorithm does not optimize the CHN selection or improve the ACO algorithm, and the DUCS algorithm does not consider the optimal paths from CHNs to the SN. Hence, they are inferior to the proposed ACOCR algorithm.

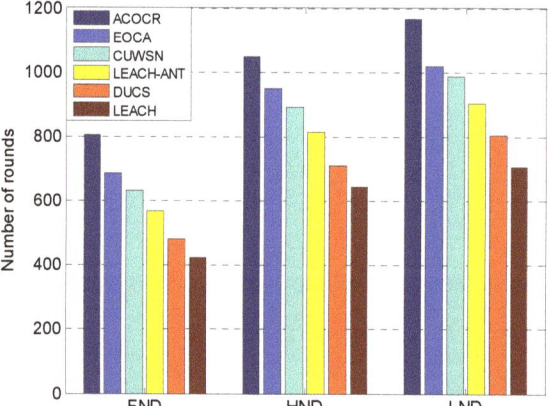

Figure 5. The number of rounds when first node dead (FND), half of the nodes dead (HND), and last node dead (LND) arise for the six algorithms.

5.2. Comparison and Analysis of the Energy Consumption of the Network

Figure 6 illustrates the total energy consumption versus the number of rounds for the six algorithms when 400 nodes were considered in the network, from which we can see that the total energy consumption rises with the increase in the network rounds regardless of which algorithm is used. However, the proposed ACOCR algorithm is the most efficient one in reducing the energy consumption. For example, in round 600, the total consumed energy of the ACOCR, EOCA, CUWSN, LEACH-ANT, DUCS, and LEACH accounts for 32.5%, 41.1%, 50.6%, 58.2%, 65.4%, and 83.8% of the initial energy of the network, respectively. As for the network energy that is completely consumed, the energy efficiency of the ACOCR is improved by 14.7%, 18.3%, 29.3%, 45.3%, and 65.2% compared to that of the EOCA, CUWSN, LEACH-ANT, DUCS, and LEACH, respectively. This is because the proposed ACOCR optimizes CHN selection and employs the optimal paths found by the improved ACO algorithm to transmit the data packets, thereby minimizing the energy consumption. The EOCA and the CUWSN outperform the LEACH, DUCS, and LEACH-ANT. However, both of them are inferior to the ACOCR, which is because neither of them optimizes the multi-hop paths for data transmission.

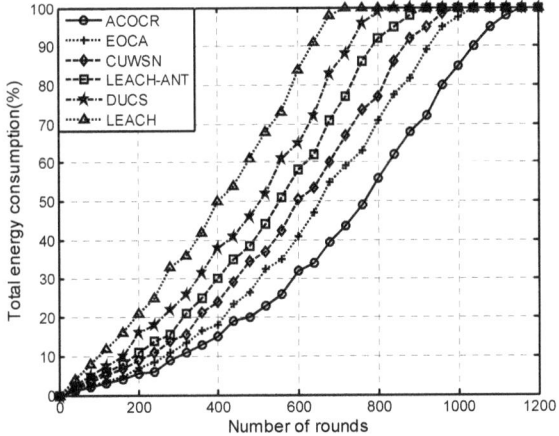

Figure 6. The total energy consumption versus the number of rounds for the six algorithms.

Figure 7 demonstrates the number of rounds when the network energy is exhausted versus the different number of nodes in the network for the six algorithms, which validates the effect of the different number of network nodes on energy consumption. As the number of nodes increases, the number of rounds when the network energy is exhausted also increases. This is because more nodes in the network lead to a better balance of energy consumption. The proposed ACOCR outperforms the other five algorithms in all situations. For example, when there are 450 nodes in the network, the ACOCR algorithm is 10.1%, 15.6%, 19.2%, 43.4%, and 52.9% more efficient than the EOCA algorithm, the CUWSN algorithm, the LEACH-ANT algorithm, the DUCS algorithm, and the LEACH algorithm, respectively.

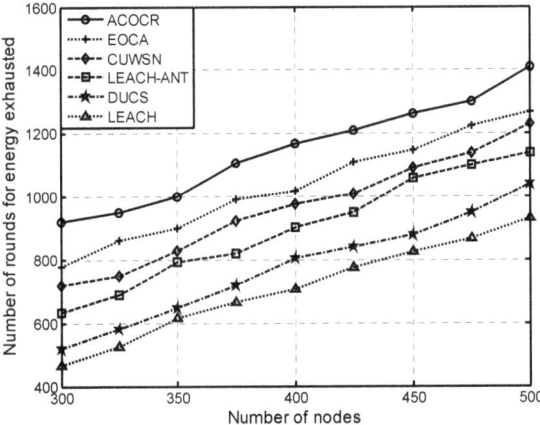

Figure 7. The number of rounds when energy is exhausted versus the number of nodes for the six algorithms.

5.3. Comparison and Analysis of the Packet Loss Ratio

Table 2 provides the packet loss ratio after round 1200 for the six algorithms when 400 nodes were considered in the network. The packet loss ratio is defined in this paper as the ratio of the number of data packets that the CHNs send to the number of data packets that the SN receives during the whole simulation process. As we can see from the table, the packet loss ratio of the proposed ACOCR is the lowest. The LEACH, which performs the worst, has about a 1.62 times higher packet loss ratio than the proposed ACOCR does. This is because the ACOCR adopts the improved ACO algorithm to find the optimal routing paths, which can reduce the risk of packet loss.

Table 2. The packet loss ratio for the six algorithms.

Algorithms	Packet Loss Ratio
ant colony optimization clustering routing (ACOCR)	12.8%
energy optimization clustering algorithm (EOCA)	14.9%
cluster-based underwater wireless sensor network (CUWSN)	15.8%
low-energy adaptive clustering hierarchy based on ant colony (LEACH-ANT)	17.1%
distributed underwater clustering scheme (DUCS)	18.8%
low-energy adaptive clustering hierarchy (LEACH)	20.7%

Figure 8 demonstrates the received packets by the SN versus the number of rounds for the six algorithms when 400 nodes were considered in the network. The more packets the SN receives, the more efficient the algorithm is. Apparently, the ACOCR algorithm has the best performance, the efficiency of which is 18.6%, 27.4%, 44.1%, 60.9%, and 84.1% higher than that of the EOCA, CUWSN, LEACH-ANT, DUCS, and LEACH, respectively, in round 1200.

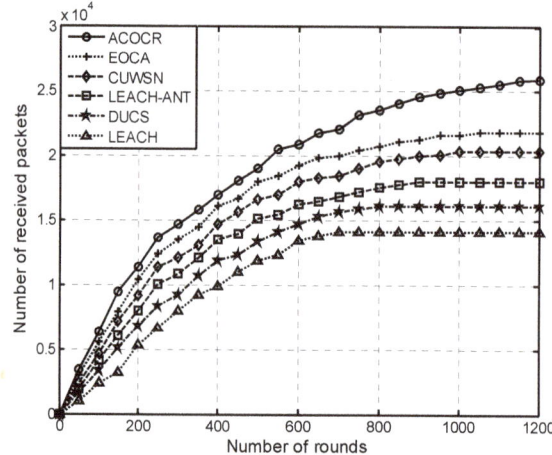

Figure 8. The number of received packets versus the number of rounds for the six algorithms.

6. Conclusions

To alleviate the problem of energy consumption in UWSNs, this paper presented an energy-efficient clustering routing algorithm based on the improved ACO algorithm. The contributions of the paper were as follows. Firstly, the improvement of the heuristic information was proposed in the paper based on the consideration of the residual energy of nodes and the distance factor. Secondly, this paper provided the improved adaptive strategy of the evaporation parameter for the pheromone update mechanism, which can be of help to the global search ability and the convergence rate of the algorithm. Thirdly, this paper proposed the ant searching scope. Fourthly, we optimized the CHN selection by considering the residual energy of nodes, the distance from the node to the SN, and the average distance between the node and the other nodes in the cube. Finally, simulation results demonstrated that the proposed ACOCR algorithm outperforms the LEACH, the DUCS, the LEACH-ANT, the CUWSN, and the EOCA in terms of the network lifetime, the energy consumption, and the packet loss ratio. The limitation of the paper is that the multipath effect of underwater channels was not considered. Therefore, we plan to study the multipath effect on the data packet transmission and design cross-layer protocols in the future. Moreover, in this paper, we employed a random method to generate the network node. In order to make the network model closer to the practical situation, we plan to use NS-3 to simulate our algorithm and call the function to generate the nodes as well as set attributes for them.

Author Contributions: Conceptualization, X.X. and H.H.; methodology, X.X.; software, X.X.; validation, X.X. and H.H.; formal analysis, X.X.; investigation, X.X.; resources, X.X.; data curation, X.X.; writing—original draft preparation, X.X.; writing—review and editing, X.X.; visualization, X.X.; supervision, H.H.; funding acquisition, H.H. All authors have read and agreed to the published version of the manuscript.

Funding: This research was funded by the National Key R&D Program of China, grant number 2018YFC1405904.

Conflicts of Interest: The authors declare no conflict of interest.

References

1. Harb, H.; Makhoul, A.; Couturier, R. An enhanced k-means and ANOVA-based clustering approach for similarity aggregation in underwater wireless sensor networks. *IEEE Sens. J.* **2015**, *15*, 5483–5493. [CrossRef]
2. Jouhari, M.; Ibrahimi, K.; Tembine, H.; Ben-Othman, J. Underwater wireless sensor networks: A survey on enabling technologies, localization protocols, and internet of underwater things. *IEEE Access* **2019**, *7*, 96879–96899. [CrossRef]
3. Rossi, P.S.; Ciuonzo, D.; Ekman, T.; Dong, H. Energy detection for MIMO decision fusion in underwater sensor networks. *IEEE Sens. J.* **2015**, *15*, 1630–1640. [CrossRef]
4. Yahya, A.; Islam, S.U.; Zahid, M.; Ahmed, G.; Raza, M.; Pervaiz, H.; Yang, F. Cooperative routing for energy efficient underwater wireless sensor networks. *IEEE Access* **2019**, *7*, 141888–141899. [CrossRef]
5. Bouabdallah, F.; Zidi, C.; Boutaba, R. Joint routing and energy management in underwater acoustic sensor networks. *IEEE Trans. Netw. Serv. Manag.* **2017**, *14*, 456–471. [CrossRef]
6. Zhou, Z.; Peng, Z.; Cui, J.; Jiang, Z. Handling triple hidden terminal problems for multichannel MAC in long-delay underwater sensor networks. *IEEE Trans. Mob. Comput.* **2012**, *11*, 139–154. [CrossRef]
7. Zhou, Y.; Yang, H.; Hu, Y.; Kung, S. Cross-layer network lifetime maximization in underwater wireless sensor networks. *IEEE Syst. J.* **2020**, *14*, 220–231. [CrossRef]
8. Wang, K.; Gao, H.; Xu, X.; Jiang, J.; Yue, D. An energy-efficient reliable data transmission scheme for complex environmental monitoring in underwater acoustic sensor networks. *IEEE Sens. J.* **2016**, *16*, 4051–4062. [CrossRef]
9. Wang, Z.; Han, G.; Qin, H.; Zhang, S.; Sui, Y. An energy-aware and void-avoidable routing protocol for underwater sensor networks. *IEEE Access* **2018**, *6*, 7792–7801. [CrossRef]
10. Xing, G.; Chen, Y.; He, L.; Su, W.; Hou, R.; Li, W.; Zhang, C.; Chen, X. Energy consumption in relay underwater acoustic sensor networks for NDN. *IEEE Access* **2019**, *7*, 42694–42702. [CrossRef]
11. Yu, W.; Chen, Y.; Wan, L.; Zhang, X.; Zhu, P.; Xu, X. An energy optimization clustering scheme for multi-hop underwater acoustic cooperative sensor networks. *IEEE Access* **2020**, *8*, 89171–89184. [CrossRef]
12. Ahmed, G.; Zhao, X.; Fareed, M.M.S.; Fareed, M.Z. An energy-efficient redundant transmission control clustering approach for underwater acoustic networks. *Sensors* **2019**, *19*, 4241. [CrossRef] [PubMed]
13. Li, X.; Fang, S.; Zhang, Y. The Study on Clustering Algorithm of the Underwater Acoustic Sensor Networks. In Proceedings of the 14th International Conference on Mechatronics and Machine Vision in Practice, Xiamen, China, 4–6 December 2007; pp. 78–81. [CrossRef]
14. Zhang, J.; Cai, M.; Han, G.; Qian, Y.; Shu, L. Cellular clustering-based interference-aware data transmission protocol for underwater acoustic sensor networks. *IEEE Trans. Veh. Technol.* **2020**, *69*, 3217–3230. [CrossRef]
15. Dang, H.; Wu, H. Clustering and cluster-based routing protocol for delay-tolerant mobile networks. *IEEE Trans. Wirel. Commun.* **2010**, *9*, 1874–1881. [CrossRef]

16. Hou, R.; He, L.; Hu, S.; Luo, J. Energy-balanced unequal layering clustering in underwater acoustic sensor networks. *IEEE Access* **2018**, *6*, 39685–39691. [CrossRef]
17. Oudani, H.; Laassiri, J.; Krit, S.; Maimouni, L.E. Comparative Study and Simulation of Flat and Hierarchical Routing Protocols for Wireless Sensor Network. In Proceedings of the 2016 International Conference on Engineering & MIS (ICEMIS), Agadir, Morocco, 22–24 September 2016; pp. 1–9. [CrossRef]
18. Heinzelman, W.R.; Chandrakasan, A.; Balakrishnan, H. Energy-Efficient Communication Protocol for Wireless Microsensor Networks. In Proceedings of the 33rd Annual Hawaii International Conference on System Sciences, Maui, HI, USA, 4–7 January 2000; pp. 3005–3014. [CrossRef]
19. Domingo, M.C. A distributed energy-aware routing protocol for underwater wireless sensor networks. *Wirel. Pers. Commun.* **2011**, *57*, 607–627. [CrossRef]
20. Xu, Y.; Yue, Z.; Lv, L. Clustering routing algorithm and simulation of internet of things perception layer based on energy balance. *IEEE Access* **2019**, *7*, 145667–145676. [CrossRef]
21. Wang, C.; Zhang, Y.; Wang, X.; Zhang, Z. Hybrid multihop partition-based clustering routing protocol for WSNs. *IEEE Sens. Lett.* **2018**, *2*, 1–4. [CrossRef]
22. Wan, Z.; Liu, S.; Ni, W.; Xu, Z. An energy-efficient multi-level adaptive clustering routing algorithm for underwater wireless sensor networks. *Clust. Comput.* **2019**, *22*, 14651–14660. [CrossRef]
23. Bhattacharjya, K.; Alam, S.; De, D. CUWSN: Energy efficient routing protocol selection for cluster based underwater wireless sensor network. *Microsyst. Technol.* **2019**. [CrossRef]
24. Ayaz, M.; Baig, I.; Abdullah, A.; Faye, I. A survey on routing techniques in underwater wireless sensor networks. *J. Netw. Comput. Appl.* **2011**, *34*, 1908–1927. [CrossRef]
25. Wang, P.; Li, C.; Zheng, J. Distributed Minimum-Cost Clustering Protocol for Underwater Sensor Networks (UWSNs). In Proceedings of the IEEE International Conference on Communications (ICC '07), Glasgow, UK, 24–28 June 2007; pp. 3510–3515. [CrossRef]
26. Ayaz, M.; Abdullah, A.; Jung, L.T. Temporary Cluster Based Routing for Underwater Wireless Sensor Networks. In Proceedings of the International Symposium in Information Technology-Engineering Technology (ITSim), Lumpur, Malaysia, 15–17 June 2010; pp. 1009–1014. [CrossRef]
27. Anupama, K.R.; Sasidharan, A.; Vadlamani, S. A Location-Based Clustering Algorithm for Data Gathering in 3D Underwater Wireless Sensor Networks. In Proceedings of the International Symposium on Telecommunications, (IST), Tehran, Iran, 27–28 August 2008; pp. 343–348. [CrossRef]
28. Seah, W.K.G.; Tan, H.P. Multipath Virtual Sink Architecture for Wireless Sensor Networks in Harsh Environments. In Proceedings of the First International Conference on Integrated Internet Ad hoc and Sensor Networks, Nice, France, 30–31 May 2006. [CrossRef]
29. Lee, U.; Wang, P.; Noh, Y.; Vieira, L.F.M.; Gerla, M.; Cui, J. Pressure Routing for Underwater Sensor Networks. In Proceedings of the IEEE INFOCOM, San Diego, CA, USA, 14–19 March 2010. [CrossRef]
30. Zhang, W.; Wang, J.; Han, G.; Zhang, X.; Feng, Y. A cluster sleep-wake scheduling algorithm based on 3D topology control in underwater sensor networks. *Sensors* **2019**, *19*, 156. [CrossRef] [PubMed]
31. Rakotomamonjy, A.; Koco, S.; Ralaivola, L. Greedy methods, randomization approaches, and multiarm bandit algorithms for efficient sparsity-constrained optimization. *IEEE Trans. Neural Netw. Learn. Syst.* **2019**, *28*, 2789–2802. [CrossRef] [PubMed]
32. Zhou, J.; Zhao, X.; Zhang, X.; Zhao, D.; Li, H. Task allocation for multi-agent systems based on distributed many-objective evolutionary algorithm and greedy algorithm. *IEEE Access* **2020**, *8*, 19306–19318. [CrossRef]
33. Saito, Y.; Nonomura, T.; Nankai, K.; Yamada, K.; Asai, K.; Sasaki, Y.; Tsubakino, D. Data-driven vector-measurement-sensor selection based on greedy algorithm. *IEEE Sens. Lett.* **2020**, *4*, 1–4. [CrossRef]
34. Lee, D.C. Proof of a modified Dijkstra's algorithm for computing shortest bundle delay in networks with deterministically time-varying links. *IEEE Commun. Lett.* **2006**, *10*, 734–736. [CrossRef]
35. Gnana Swathika, O.V.; Hemamalini, S. Prims-aided Dijkstra algorithm for adaptive protection in microgrids. *IEEE J. Emerg. Sel. Top. Power Electron.* **2016**, *4*, 1279–1286. [CrossRef]
36. Luo, M.; Hou, X.; Yang, J. Surface optimal path planning using an extended Dijkstra algorithm. *IEEE Access* **2020**, *8*, 147827–147838. [CrossRef]
37. Xia, P.; Xia, Z.; Hongyi, Y.; Chao, Z. Study on Routing Protocol for WSNs Based on the Improved Prim Algorithm. In Proceedings of the 2009 International Conference on Wireless Communications & Signal Processing, Nanjing, China, 13–15 November 2009; pp. 1–4. [CrossRef]

38. Feo, T.A.; Resende, M.G.C. Greedy randomized adaptive search procedures. *J. Glob. Optim.* **1995**, *6*, 109–133. [CrossRef]
39. Jovanovic, R.; Stefan, V. The fixed set search applied to the power dominating set problem. *Expert Syst.* **2020**. [CrossRef]
40. Arnaout, J.P. A worm optimization algorithm to minimize the makespan on unrelated parallel machines with sequence-dependent setup times. *Ann. Oper. Res.* **2020**, *285*, 273–293. [CrossRef]
41. Krishnaswamy, V.; Manvi, S.S. Fuzzy and PSO based clustering scheme in underwater acoustic sensor networks using energy and distance parameters. *Wirel. Pers. Commun.* **2019**, *108*, 1529–1546. [CrossRef]
42. Zhang, X.; Shen, X.; Yu, Z. A novel hybrid ant colony optimization for a multicast routing problem. *Algorithms* **2019**, *12*, 18. [CrossRef]
43. Liu, X. Routing protocols based on ant colony optimization in wireless sensor networks: A survey. *IEEE Access* **2017**, *5*, 26303–26317. [CrossRef]
44. Stodola, P. Using metaheuristics on the multi-depot vehicle routing problem with modified optimization criterion. *Algorithms* **2018**, *11*, 74. [CrossRef]
45. Lv, J.; Wang, X.; Huang, M. Ant colony optimization-inspired ICN routing with content concentration and similarity relation. *IEEE Commun. Lett.* **2017**, *21*, 1313–1316. [CrossRef]
46. Li, X.; Keegan, B.; Mtenzi, F.; Weise, T.; Tan, M. Energy-efficient load balancing ant based routing algorithm for wireless sensor networks. *IEEE Access* **2019**, *7*, 113182–113196. [CrossRef]
47. Agarwal, T.; Kumar, D.; Prakash, N.R. Prolonging Network Lifetime Using Ant Colony Optimization Algorithm on Leach Protocol for Wireless Sensor Networks. In Proceedings of the 2nd International Conference on Networks and Communications, Chennai, India, 23–25 July 2010; pp. 634–641. [CrossRef]
48. Okdem, S.; Karaboga, D. Routing in Wireless Sensor Networks Using Ant Colony Optimization. In Proceedings of the First NASA/ESA Conference on Adaptive Hardware and Systems (AHS'06), Istanbul, Turkey, 15–18 June 2006; pp. 401–404. [CrossRef]
49. Camilo, T.; Carreto, C.; Silva, J.S.; Boavida, F. An Energy-Efficient Ant-Based Routing Algorithm for Wireless Sensor Networks. In Proceedings of the 5th International Workshop on Ant Colony Optimization and Swarm Intelligence, Brussels, Belgium, 4–7 September 2006; pp. 49–59.
50. Shan, Y. Study on Submarine Path Planning Based on Modified Ant Colony Optimization Algorithm. In Proceedings of the 2018 IEEE International Conference on Mechatronics and Automation (ICMA), Changchun, China, 5–8 August 2018; pp. 288–292. [CrossRef]
51. Zhang, T.; Chen, G.; Zeng, Q.; Song, G.; Li, C.; Duan, H. Routing clustering protocol for 3d wireless sensor networks based on fragile collection ant colony algorithm. *IEEE Access* **2020**, *8*, 58874–58888. [CrossRef]
52. Sun, Y.; Dong, W.; Chen, Y. An improved routing algorithm based on ant colony optimization in wireless sensor networks. *IEEE Commun. Lett.* **2017**, *21*, 1317–1320. [CrossRef]
53. Liu, X. A transmission scheme for wireless sensor networks using ant colony optimization with unconventional characteristics. *IEEE Commun. Lett.* **2014**, *18*, 1214–1217. [CrossRef]
54. Han, G.; Jiang, J.; Shu, L.; Xu, Y.; Wang, F. Localization algorithms of underwater wireless sensor networks: A survey. *Sensors* **2012**, *12*, 2026–2061. [CrossRef] [PubMed]
55. Sozer, E.M.; Stojanovic, M.; Proakis, J.G. Underwater acoustic networks. *IEEE J. Ocean. Eng.* **2000**, *25*, 72–83. [CrossRef]
56. Dorigo, M.; Maniezzo, V.; Colorni, A. Ant system: Optimization by a colony of cooperating agents. *IEEE Trans. Syst. Man Cybern. Part B Cybern.* **1996**, *26*, 29–41. [CrossRef] [PubMed]
57. Dorigo, M.; Gambardella, L.M. Ant colony system: A cooperative learning approach to the traveling salesman problem. *IEEE Trans. Evol. Comput.* **1997**, *1*, 53–66. [CrossRef]
58. Stützle, T.; Hoos, H.H. MAX–MIN ant system. *Future Gener. Comput. Syst.* **2000**, *16*, 889–914. [CrossRef]
59. Jovanovic, R.; Tuba, M. An ant colony optimization algorithm with improved pheromone correction strategy for the minimum weight vertex cover problem. *Appl. Soft Comput. J.* **2011**, *11*, 5360–5366. [CrossRef]

© 2020 by the authors. Licensee MDPI, Basel, Switzerland. This article is an open access article distributed under the terms and conditions of the Creative Commons Attribution (CC BY) license (http://creativecommons.org/licenses/by/4.0/).

Article

Citywide Cellular Traffic Prediction Based on a Hybrid Spatiotemporal Network

Dehai Zhang *, Linan Liu, Cheng Xie, Bing Yang and Qing Liu

School of Software, Yunnan University, Kunming 650504, China; liulinan@mail.ynu.edu.cn (L.L.); xiecheng@ynu.edu.cn (C.X.); yang.bing@mail.ynu.edu.cn (B.Y.); liuqing@ynu.edu.cn (Q.L.)
* Correspondence: dhzhang@ynu.edu.cn

Received: 27 November 2019; Accepted: 6 January 2020; Published: 8 January 2020

Abstract: With the arrival of 5G networks, cellular networks are moving in the direction of diversified, broadband, integrated, and intelligent networks. At the same time, the popularity of various smart terminals has led to an explosive growth in cellular traffic. Accurate network traffic prediction has become an important part of cellular network intelligence. In this context, this paper proposes a deep learning method for space-time modeling and prediction of cellular network communication traffic. First, we analyze the temporal and spatial characteristics of cellular network traffic from Telecom Italia. On this basis, we propose a hybrid spatiotemporal network (HSTNet), which is a deep learning method that uses convolutional neural networks to capture the spatiotemporal characteristics of communication traffic. This work adds deformable convolution to the convolution model to improve predictive performance. The time attribute is introduced as auxiliary information. An attention mechanism based on historical data for weight adjustment is proposed to improve the robustness of the module. We use the dataset of Telecom Italia to evaluate the performance of the proposed model. Experimental results show that compared with the existing statistics methods and machine learning algorithms, HSTNet significantly improved the prediction accuracy based on MAE and RMSE.

Keywords: communication traffic prediction; intelligent traffic management; deformable convolution; attention mechanism

1. Introduction

With the advent of fifth-generation mobile networks (5G), the cellular Internet of Things (IoT) has become a popular topic in industry [1,2]. The Groupe Speciale Mobile Association (GSMA) predicted that by 2020, the number of IoT connections will exceed 30 billion, and the number of connections based on cellular technology will reach one to two billion. The current 4G wireless network has greatly affected our lives, and the stable communication system brought by the future 5G will become a powerful promoter of Industry 4.0 [3–5]. Real-time and secure data transmission is an important guarantee for Industry 4.0, and 5G has the characteristics of large transmission data, high security, and short delay time.

At the same time, the explosive growth of global mobile devices and the IoT has also accelerated the era of big data [6,7]. Communication equipment plays an increasingly important role in people's daily lives, such as sensing, communication, entertainment, and work. A large number of communication services have generated countless mobile data; the wireless cellular networks carrying the data have become increasingly advanced and complex; and a large quantity of real-time system operation data is generated every moment. To realize intelligent management of cellular networks, it is very important to perform real-time or non-real-time regular analysis and accurate prediction of cellular traffic. For example, accurate prediction of future traffic can greatly increase the efficiency of demand aware resource allocation [8].

However, cellular network traffic changes have elusive rules, and the variation in traffic in a particular region is strongly correlated with many external factors, such as business, location, time, and user lifestyle. To extract more effectively the changing characteristics of cellular network traffic, many related studies have been carried out. The existing methods can be divided into two types: statistical or probabilistic methods and machine learning methods.

For the first kind of methods, this includes the autoregressive integrated moving average (ARIMA) [9,10], α-stable distribution [11], and covariance function [12]. In the traffic prediction problem, these methods have comprehensively studied the characteristics of cellular networks and have shown that changes in communication traffic have both temporal autocorrelation and spatial autocorrelation. However, as the communication modes of cellular networks become more complex and subject to many external factors, these traditional linear statistical methods are not suitable for current communication traffic prediction problems.

With the development of artificial intelligence technology, machine learning methods have been widely used in industry and have also been used for cellular network traffic prediction in recent years [13]. Early researchers proposed using linear regression [14] and SVM regression [15] to predict cellular traffic. Many studies have also proposed methods for traffic prediction based on deep learning. In [16], the authors proposed a deep learning based prediction method to simulate the long term dependence of cellular network traffic in 2017. The method mainly uses self-encoded depth models and long short term memory cells (LSTM) for space-time modeling. However, the processing of self-encoding will lose some of the original information, and the ability to extract spatial features needs to be improved. In 2018, Zhang et al. [17] proposed a cellular traffic prediction method based on a convolutional neural network (STDenseNet); however, this method did not consider the impact of external conditions on traffic prediction, and the traditional convolution method had a limited effect on the complex spatial characteristics of cellular traffic.

Motivated by the aforementioned problems, based on STDenseNet, this work proposes a new hybrid spatiotemporal network (HSTNet). First, the deformable convolution unit is used in the model to improve the ability to extract complex spatial features. Then, time characteristics are introduced to enhance the accuracy of traffic prediction. Finally, an attention mechanism based on traffic history data is proposed to further enhance the robustness of the model.

2. Data Observation and Analysis

The wireless communication data analyzed in this paper were from Telecom Italia, which is the traffic statistics sent or received by users in specific areas of Milan [18]. The dataset consisted of a time series of traffic from 1 November 2013 to 1st January 2014, with an interval of 10 min, and included three parts: short message service (SMS), call service (Call), and Internet access (Internet). The entire urban area was divided into cells of size $H \times W$. H and W represent the number of rows and columns of cells. In this dataset, $H = W = 100$, indicating that the area of Milan is composed of a grid overlay of 10,000 cells with a size of about 235×235 square meters, and the value of the cell represents the statistical value of the traffic in and out of this area. Traffic data were recorded from 00:00 11/01/2013 to 23:59 01/01/2014. We merged data at ten minute intervals into hour intervals and divided each dataset into 1488 (62 days × 24 h) fragments. In the datasets, SMS and Call contained two dimensions of traffic, namely receiving and sending. The Internet only recorded the traffic that was accessed. In order to compare the spatiotemporal characteristics of the traffic of the three services clearly, we combined the traffic of the receiving and sending dimensions into one.

Thus, the entire dataset could be represented as data of $[c, t, H, W]$ dimensions $F_{c,t}$ where c represents the type of cellular traffic in the dataset, $c \in \{SMS, Call, Internet\}$. t represents the time interval of the flow, and $t = 1$ h in this work. H and W are as described above.

$$\mathbf{F}_{c,t} = \begin{bmatrix} f_{c,t}^{(1,1)} & f_{c,t}^{(1,2)} & \cdots & f_{c,t}^{(1,W)} \\ f_{c,t}^{(2,1)} & f_{c,t}^{(2,2)} & \cdots & f_{c,t}^{(2,H)} \\ \vdots & \vdots & \ddots & \vdots \\ f_{c,t}^{(H,1)} & f_{c,t}^{(H,2)} & \cdots & f_{c,t}^{(H,W)} \end{bmatrix} \quad (1)$$

where $f_{c,t}^{(H,W)}$ represents the traffic statistics of the cell (H, W) of the traffic data of type c at time t.

2.1. Temporal Domain

Figure 1 shows the trends in three different traffic flows over a 48 h period; from top to bottom, SMS, Call, and Internet. From the picture, we can clearly find that the three different traffics were subjected to a strong daily time change pattern. Basically, the traffic started to increase at approximately eight o'clock in the morning and then stayed above a very high level and started to fall at approximately eight o'clock in the evening. There were also significant differences between different traffics. The Internet traffic remained constant even at night, and Call and SMS were mostly concentrated during the day. These rules clearly correspond with the daily lives of people. Compared to daytime work and life, people make very few SMS messages and calls at night. However, the Internet not only provides contact needs, but automatic access equipment, entertainment, and other factors will lead to a large number of Internet accesses at night. Therefore, the day and night trend is relatively small compared to SMS and Call.

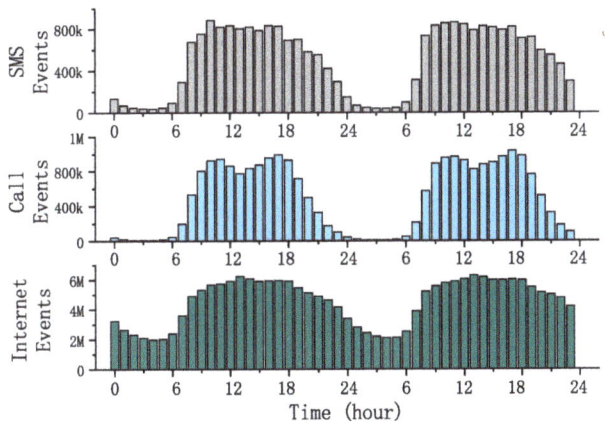

Figure 1. Hourly traffic change statistics.

Figure 2 is the dynamic graph of the daily total traffic in November 2013. The three types of traffic had obvious differences on working days and holidays, and the traffic on holidays was much lower than that on working days, which showed whether it was a working day that had an important impact on daily traffic. For example, the first day in the picture is an Italian legal holiday, and the second and third days are the weekend; the total traffic on these three days was significantly less than the next five working days.

Comparing the changes in the three types of traffic on weekdays and holidays, we found that the gap of Call traffic on the two dates was considerable, and the working day traffic was generally close to twice the holiday traffic. SMS traffic trends were smaller than Call, but the gap was also large. The reason was obvious: users needed to communicate more during the working day. Similar to the statistical rule of Figure 1, the daily traffic trend of the Internet was smaller than SMS and Call.

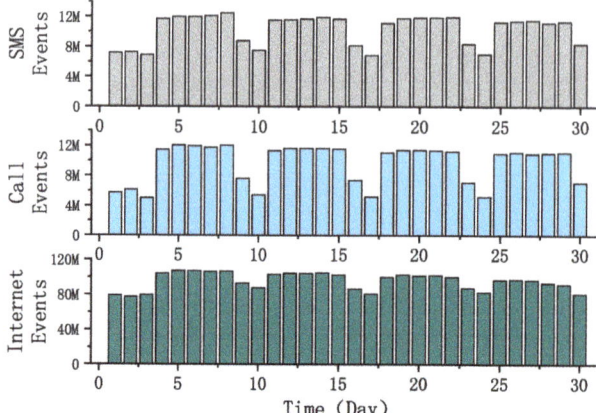

Figure 2. Daily traffic change statistics.

2.2. Spatial Domain

Figure 3 shows the spatial distribution of Call traffic over a certain period of time. We can easily find that the traffic distribution of the whole city was very uneven. Intensive traffic was concentrated in the downtown area, while urban suburbs had very sparse traffic distributions. Moreover, it can be clearly seen from Figure 3 that a few areas covered traffic much higher than other areas. These areas were usually the bustling areas of the city and were often the most burdensome areas for wireless networks, and accurate predictions of traffic in these areas are important. However, these areas carrying large amounts of traffic also pose great difficulties for traffic prediction modeling. The existence of such singular values was very detrimental to the fitting of the model. Moreover, the trend of traffic fluctuations in these areas was often much larger than in other areas, and more research is needed to capture its space-time characteristics well.

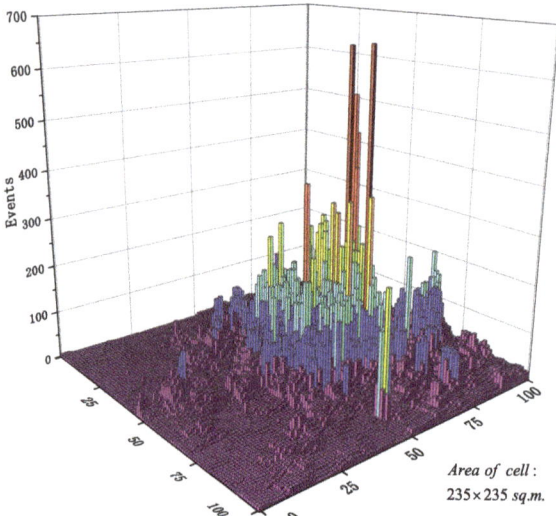

Figure 3. Spatial distribution of cellular network traffic.

The correlation between traffic changes in different cells cannot be seen intuitively through Figure 3. To better show the spatial correlation of cellular traffic, we extracted 11 × 11 cells in the Call dataset for correlation analysis. Figure 4 shows the Pearson correlation coefficient ρ for the spatial correlation between target cell $x^{(i,j)}$ and its neighboring cells $x^{(i',j')}$. The Pearson correlation coefficient is a widely used metric [16,17]. Its definition is expressed as follows:

$$\rho = \frac{\text{cov}\left(x^{(i,j)}, x^{(i',j')}\right)}{\sigma_{x^{(i,j)}} \sigma_{x^{(i',j')}}} \tag{2}$$

where cov represents the covariance operator and σ represents the standard deviation. Figure 4 shows that the spatial correlation between different urban areas depended not only on the their proximity, but also on many external factors. For example, Cell (3,4) was the same distance from cell (4,3) to target cell (5,5), but the correlation coefficient was very different (0.35 and 0.96). Generally, the change in traffic was not necessarily highly related to neighboring cells and may also be strongly related to non-adjacent cells. However, the traditional convolution can only extract the information of neighboring cells. Therefore, we needed to find new ways to get potentially relevant information.

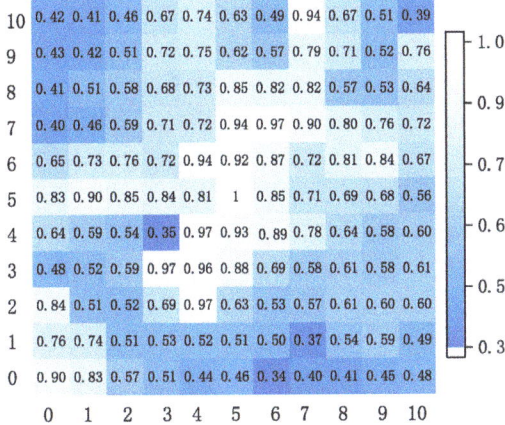

Figure 4. Spatial correlation analysis.

3. Cellular Traffic Prediction Model

3.1. Model Framework Introduction

This section mainly introduces our proposed hybrid spatiotemporal network HSTNet, which is mainly based on STDenseNet. HSTNet consists of two input sections and three module sections. The three modules include the convolution module, the time-embedding module, and the attention module. The predicted value $P^{(h,w)}$ of the model was combined with the output data of the three modules. The model framework is shown in Figure 5.

The traffic of each time period in the datasets was counted by 100 × 100 cells; that is, the traffic data of each time period could be composed of a 100 × 100 traffic distribution matrix. Therefore, we could effectively extract the spatial correlation of cellular traffic through convolutional neural networks. The main prediction module of our model was also implemented by the improved solution of the convolutional neural network (DenseNet) [19]. The historical data included the last three time periods and the current time period of the previous three days. We considered that cellular traffic was not only highly correlated with the traffic distribution of the previous few hours, but also depended on the traffic distribution at the current moment of the previous few days. Therefore, we entered the two pieces of historical data into the model separately. For example, if we forecast the traffic at 12 o'clock on the 11th of a certain month, the input data were the traffic data of 12 h on 8/9/10 of the month and the traffic data of 9/10/11 o'clock on the day. After the historical data were entered into the model, they were processed by two modules: the convolution module and the attention module. The convolution module consisted of two DenseNets with deformable convolutions [20] that handled the historical data of the two parts. The output matrix was fused through a matrix of learnable parameters.

In the second section, we analyzed the time correlation of cellular traffic data. There were strong correlations with cellular traffic at different times of the day and whether it was a holiday. The input data of the time embedding module included the hour value of the predicted time and the attribute of the date (working day or holiday). The matrix generated by the time embedding module would be added to the matrix output by the convolution module.

The attention module received the input of two historical data items and performed integration operations. Then, a weight matrix based on historical data was output. The matrix adjusted the weight of the output of the first two modules and output $O^{(h,w)}$. Finally, the final prediction matrix $P'^{(h,w)}$ was output through the sigmoid function and compared with the real value $P^{(h,w)}$.

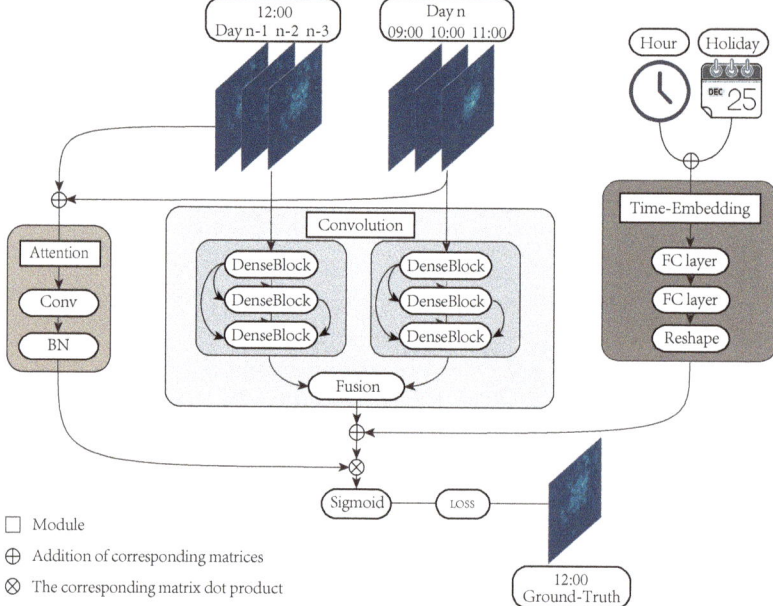

Figure 5. The hybrid spatiotemporal network's (HSTNet) framework structure.

3.2. Convolution Module

In recent years, the improvement of convolutional neural network performance has been mainly divided into two major areas. One area is depth, such as ResNet, which solves the problem of gradient disappearance when the network is too deep [21]. The other area is the width, such as the Inception network, which uses a multi-scale convolution kernel to extend the model's generalization capabilities. In STDenseNet, the prediction module consists of two densely concatenated convolutional networks with the same structure. Similar to ResNet, DenseNet also establishes a dense connection between the front and back layers; that is, each layer accepts the output of all the previous layers as input and implements feature reuse in turn. DenseNet relies on the ultimate use of the network architecture to achieve fewer parameters and leading performance compared to traditional models [19].

Cellular traffic has a strong spatiotemporal autocorrelation. This work uses DenseNet to extract the spatiotemporal features of historical data, which can achieve better results than the traditional single channel convolutional neural network. The convolution module in HSTNet contains two separate DenseNets for processing two sets of historical data. Each DenseNet consists of three layers, each consisting of a unit block we call the DenseBlock. The outputs of the two DenseNets are multiplied by the learnable parameter matrix and then added.

3.3. Deformable Convolution

In recent years, convolutional neural networks have achieved excellent performance in many image fields with their good feature extraction ability and end-to-end learning. The convolution in the network samples different regions of the input image and then convolves the sampled information as an output. This convolution operation determines that the geometric deformation capability of the model does not come from the network, but from the diversity of the dataset. For example, assume that Q represents the receptive field area covered by the convolution kernel, in a 3×3 convolution kernel, $Q = (1,1), (1,0), \ldots, (0,1), (1,1)$. For any pixel point P_0 on the feature map, the standard convolution method is as follows:

$$y(P_0) = \sum_{P_n \in Q} W(P_n) \cdot x(P_0 + P_n) \tag{3}$$

Because the ordinary convolution method has limited adaptability to the complex spatial correlation of cellular network traffic, we introduced a deformable convolution to the model. The process of deformable convolution is to add an offset variable ΔP_n at each sampling point position. ΔP_n can be continuously learned and adaptively changed according to the current image content. This means that the convolution kernel is not limited to a fixed position sampling method, but can search for the region of interest near the current position for sampling. Thus, the convolution kernel improves the feature extraction capability for complex spaces. The following is the calculation process of the deformable convolution:

$$y(P_0) = \sum_{P_n \in Q} W(P_n) \cdot x(P_0 + P_n + \Delta P_n) \tag{4}$$

The traditional convolution window only needs to train the pixel weight parameters of each convolution window. The deformable convolutional network must add some parameters to train the shape of the convolution window, that is the offset vector of each pixel. The offset field in Figure 6 is the additional parameter to be trained, and its size is the same as the input picture size. The convolution window slides on the offset field to achieve the effect of convolution pixel offset and optimize the sampling points.

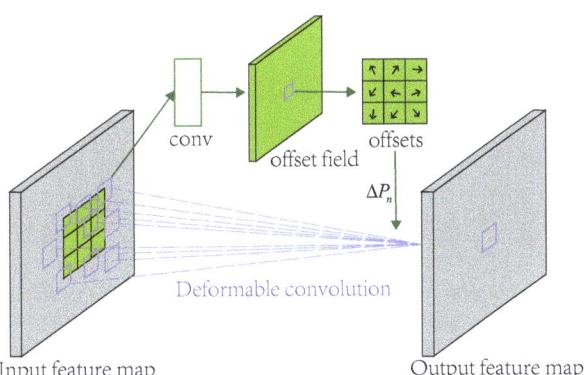

Figure 6. Illustration of a 3×3 deformable convolution.

It can be seen from the above analysis that if $\Delta P_n = 0$, the deformable convolution becomes a normal convolution, and there is no improvement in performance. In the process of predicting cellular network traffic, an ordinary convolution can only extract features for a fixed size range. The deformable convolution can extend the feature extraction range to more effective areas around by learning the offset variable ΔP_n. In this training process, the model can be offset from the area calculated by the common convolution kernel to other areas with more correlation and effectively avoids interference from uncorrelated spatial features, thus improving the predictive performance of cellular traffic.

In summary, to improve the spatial feature extraction ability of the model, a deformable convolution unit is added to each layer (DenseBlock) in the DenseNet. As shown in Figure 7, the original DenseBlock consists of a batch normalization layer, a rectified linear units (ReLU) layer, and a 3×3 convolution layer. The improvement of this paper is to change the 3×3 convolution layer to a 1×1 size, which is used to shape the data of the current DenseBlock, then access the batch normalization(BN) layer, the ReLU layer, and the deformable convolution layer in turn.

Since the traditional DenseBlock reuses the features of all previous layers, the deeper DenseBlock requires more parameters. Adding a 1×1 convolution layer can integrate input features into low dimensions and reduce the number of model parameters. We replaced the improved DenseBlock in the three-tier DenseNet, and the model parameters dropped from 230 thousand to 170 thousand. Replacing traditional convolutions with deformable convolution can expand the perceived range of convolution and improve the feature extraction capabilities of spatial features.

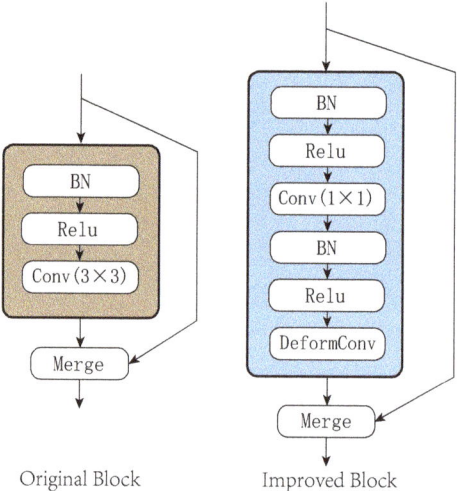

Figure 7. Improved structure of DenseBlock.

3.4. Time Embedding Module

In the previous data analysis, we can see that time had a strong correlation with communication traffic. To capture the temporal characteristics of the data for better model prediction, we collected Italian holiday information and introduced hours and holidays as external features in the model input. The specific process was as follows.

- Dividing the time period of the day into 24 segments, representing 24 h, the time attribute of each data was represented by a 24-dimensional one-hot vector (*Hour_of_Day*).
- Holiday (including weekends and Italian festivals) is represented by a one-dimensional vector (*Is_of_Holiday*) and is entered with 0 or 1, 1 indicating that the day is a holiday and 0 indicating that the day is a working day.

The above two vectors were combined into a 25-dimensional vector *T*. For example, if the predicted time point is 12:00:00 11/01/2013 (Italian holiday), the two time data *Is_of_Holiday* (1) and *Hour_of_Day* (a 24-dimensional one-hot vector, its 12th bit is 1) are extracted to form a time feature vector T. The feature vector T is input to the two layer fully connected layer, and the output is an $H \times W$ dimensional vector v_{time}. The vector is reshaped into a matrix M_{time} of $H \times W$ in size through a reshape layer and merged with the input result of the prediction branch. The reshape layer receives a vector of length $H \times W$ and shapes it into a matrix of $H \times W$. The calculation process is as follows:

$$v_{time} = \sigma \left(W_{time}^2 \sigma \left(W_{time}^1 T + b_{time}^1 \right) + b_{time}^2 \right) \tag{5}$$

where W_{time}^i and b_{time}^i are the learnable parameters of the ith fully connected layer. σ represents the sigmoid activation function.

$$M_{time} = \text{Reshape}(v_{time}) \tag{6}$$

where $v_{time} \in R^{HW \times 1}$ and $M_{time} \in R^{H \times W}$.

3.5. Attention Module

The human brain receives considerable external input information at every moment. When the human brain receives this information, it consciously or unconsciously uses the attention mechanism to obtain more important information. At present, this attention mechanism has been introduced into the fields of natural language processing, object detection, semantic segmentation, etc., and has achieved good results. In our work, an attention mechanism was added to the network as a module to optimize the density map generated by the prediction.

The statistical value of the most densely populated area is often much larger than the value of most other areas in the traffic dataset. For example, in a traffic distribution matrix, the average is 30, but the maximum is 4000. This is very disadvantageous for accurate prediction of images by convolutional neural networks. Therefore, to solve the problem that the value gap between different regions is too large in the model prediction process and improve the overall prediction performance of the model, this paper proposes a weight adjustment scheme based on an attention mechanism. The density map traffic density distribution has a strong correlation with the corresponding historical data. Therefore, we integrated the corresponding historical data as input, merged them into a two-column attention matrix through a 1×1 convolution kernel, and normalized it to form a weight matrix $W^{(h,w)}$. Then, $W^{(h,w)}$ multiplies the matrix $M^{(h,w)}$ generated by the prediction branch to generate a prediction matrix $O^{(h,w)}$ for adjusting the weights. The calculation is as follows:

$$O^{(h,w)} = W^{(h,w)} \cdot M^{(h,w)} \tag{7}$$

In this way, higher weights can be obtained for pixels with relatively higher traffic density in historical data, and lower weights can be obtained for pixels with relatively lower density. In the case, weights are differentiated from the density map generated by the prediction module. The operation can improve the quality of the final density map.

4. Experimental Results and Analysis

4.1. Experimental Process and Parameter Setting

The experimental dataset was from Telecom Italia, and we used the same pre-processing method as [17] to aggregate data from the 10 min interval in the original dataset to hours. Because the 10 min interval dataset was quite sparse, it was not conducive to extracting spatiotemporal characteristics. The difference was that [17] separately predicted the receive and send dimensions in SMS and Call. We combined the receive and send dimensions and used the total traffic input model for prediction. All data were normalized before inputting in the model, which allowed the model to converge faster and improved the computational efficiency of the fitting process.

HSTNet uses an optimization algorithm, Adam [22], which can replace the traditional stochastic gradient descent algorithm, which iteratively updates the neural network weights based on the training data. The experiment was carried out in three datasets with a learning rate of 0.01 and a training of 150 epochs. The learning rate decayed as the epoch of training increased. Our model was tested on three datasets: SMS, Call, and Internet. Each dataset contained 1488 (62 days × 24 h) slices. Except for the first three days without sufficient historical data, we used 52 days of data (1248 pieces) from 4 November 2013 to 24 December 2013 as the training set and used data from 25 December 2013 to 1 January 2014 (168 pieces) as the test set. In the convolution module, the deformable convolutional layer had 32 filters. The remaining convolutional layers had 16 filters with a kernel size of 1 × 1. The normal convolutional layer in the attention module had one filter with a kernel size of 1 × 1. The activation function of the convolutional layers was ReLU, except for the last layer, which used the sigmoid activation function. The code of HSTNet was implemented under Python 3.7, Keras 2.1.6, and NumPy 1.15.4. The experimental hardware environment included AMD R5 2600, GTX 1070, and 16 G memory.

Our experiments compared HSTNet performance with baseline algorithms such as the historical average (HA), ARIMA, LSTM, and STDenseNet. In the experiment process, the deformable convolution, time embedding module, and attention module were embedded in STDenseNet to observe the performance improvement of the model, and HSTNet had all the above improvements added. The generated prediction map was re-adjusted to the normal scale and then evaluated with the true value.

We used the two indicators of mean absolute error (MAE) and root mean squared error (RMSE) to evaluate the model. MAE is the average of the absolute error, which can better reflect the actual situation of the predicted value error.

$$MAE = \frac{\sum_{h=1}^{H} \sum_{W=1}^{W} \left| p'^{(h,w)} - p^{(h,w)} \right|}{H \times W} \tag{8}$$

RMSE represents the square root of the second sample moment of the differences between predicted values and observed values or the quadratic mean of these differences. RMSE is more sensitive to outliers.

$$RMSE = \sqrt{\frac{\sum_{h=1}^{H} \sum_{W=1}^{W} \left(p'^{(h,w)} - p^{(h,w)} \right)^2}{H \times W}} \tag{9}$$

4.2. Experiment Analysis

To compare the performance of HSTNet proposed in this paper, we selected three existing traffic prediction algorithms as the baseline of this experiment: historical average (HA), ARIMA, LSTM, and STDenseNet. Four methods performed MAE- and RMSE-based evaluations on three datasets. The result is shown in Figure 8.

From Figure 8, we can see that HSTNet's MSE and RMSE performance in the three traffic datasets was ahead of the other existing algorithms. The historical average was simply calculated from historical data and lacked the mining of deep correlations. ARIMA only considered the historical timing characteristics of the data, without regard for other dependencies. The performance of LSTM was better than statistical methods, but worse than other deep learning methods. STDenseNet did not consider the impact of external factors. Our model not only better extracted the spatial correlation of traffic data, but also considered the impact of time attributes on traffic changes, so the best performance was achieved.

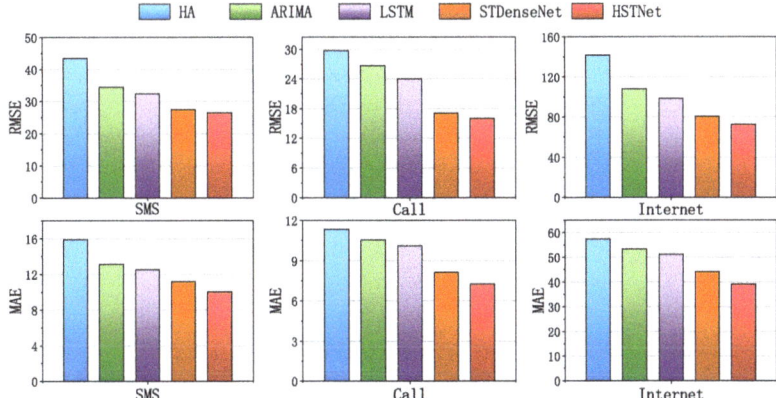

Figure 8. Comparison of prediction performance on the baseline and HSTNet. HA, historical average.

In Table 1, we calculate the model evaluation results after adding the deformable convolution, time embedding module, and attention module in STDenseNet. In Table 1, +DeformConv represents embedding only deformable convolutions in the baseline. HSTNet was evaluated after incorporating three improvements. The model achieved the best MAE and RMSE performance on Call, and the effect on SMS was slightly worse. The effect of the model on Internet improved, but the overall performance was far worse than Call and SMS because the traffic on Internet was very different from the SMS and the Call traffic. In some cases, it was close to ten times the gap. Considerable traffic changes had a large impact on model performance.

It is worth mentioning that the traffic gap between different cells after integration was about twice that of the original, which was more complicated than the separate prediction. Therefore, compared to the results in [17], our experiments obtained larger RMSE and MAE on SMS and Call.

Table 1. Overall performance of the model.

Dataset	Model	MAE	RMSE
SMS	STDenseNet	11.10	27.49
	+DeformConv	10.81	26.91
	+Time-property	10.66	27.22
	+Attention	10.09	26.62
	HSTNet	10.01	26.42
Call	STDenseNet	8.13	17.10
	+DeformConv	7.61	16.18
	+Time-property	8.03	16.89
	+Attention	7.27	16.70
	HSTNet	7.25	16.04
Internet	STDenseNet	44.15	80.51
	+DeformConv	43.23	77.75
	+Time-property	39.73	77.08
	+Attention	39.89	74.48
	HSTNet	39.19	72.72

Figure 9 shows the performance improvement of the model by adding different modules and HSTNet. For the SMS datasets, the addition of deformable convolution, time embedding, and attention modules increased by 2.61%, 3.96%, and 9.09%, respectively, the RMSE. For the MAE, there were 2.11%, 0.98%, and 3.16% performance improvements. For the Call dataset, the addition of deformable convolution units had an increase in 6.39% and 5.38% in MAE and RMSE, respectively; the attention module had a 10.57% improvement in MAE. For the Internet dataset, the three improvements we proposed still improved the results to varying degrees. The effect of adding the time attribute and the attention module was very obvious and had an approximately 10% improvement on the MAE.

It can be seen that the three different improvements improved the results in the different datasets, verifying the correctness of the hypotheses in Section 3. Different improvements had different effects on the three datasets. The attention module was very impressive for predicting the performance of all datasets. Deformable convolution and time embedding modules also had varying degrees of performance improvement for individual datasets. Overall, the performance improvement created by the attention mechanism was greater than the other two improvements.

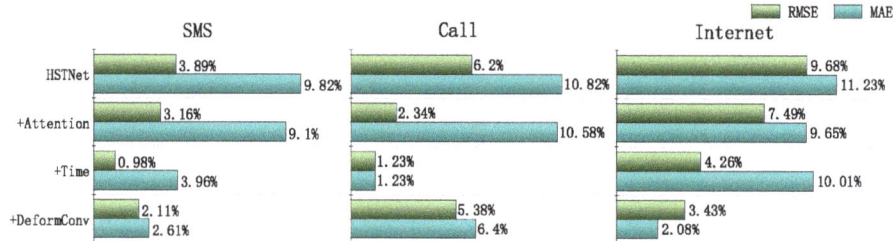

Figure 9. Comparison of different module effects based on STDenseNet.

Embedding different modules had different effects on the model's runtime and parameters. Table 2 shows the changes in the time to train an epoch and the number of parameters under different conditions. We added each module individually to observe the results. Although the time embedding module and the attention module had added parameters, they had little effect on the running time. The addition of deformable convolution reduced the parameters by about 69K, but complex calculations increased the running time by nearly half. There was no difference in the running cost of the three datasets due to the same structure.

Considering the performance and cost of HSTNet, we think that the time embedding module and attention module were the most effective strategies for improving model performance. Deformable convolution could improve prediction performance to a certain extent, but it also increased the running time of the model. It should be mentioned that DenseBlock with more filters could obtain better performance, but the training time was greatly increased. For example, if we replaced the original 32 filters with the 64 filters, we could increase the above results of RMSE by 2.3%, but nearly three times the training time in SMS.

Table 2. The effects on parameters and the time of each epoch.

Model	Time	Parameters
STDenseNet	22s	239K
+DeformConv	34s	170K
+Time-property	23s	350K
+Attention	22s	243K
HSTNet	35s	284K

In Section 3.1, we mentioned that the input data included the last three time periods and the current time period of the previous three days. We input different time dimensions to analyze the impact on HSTNet's performance. The N-dimensional data represented the data from the last N time periods and the current time period of the previous N days. As shown in Table 3, different time dimensions had a certain impact on the RMSE results. In the three datasets, HSTNet achieved the best performance when inputting three-dimensional data. The performance was slightly poorer when only one- or two-dimensional data were input, which indicated that the model could not extract the spatiotemporal characteristics of the traffic well in this case. When $N = 4$, the performance of the model would also decrease. We believe that this was caused by the introduction of more low correlation data.

Table 3. RMSE results of different input dimensions.

Input Dimension	1	2	3	4
SMS	27.51	27.18	**26.42**	26.83
Call	16.86	16.23	**16.04**	16.62
Internet	80.10	75.38	**72.72**	78.32

Figure 10 shows the cell of the Internet dataset (55,58), the predicted values of the five methods compared to the real values. To visually show the difference in performance, we compared their accumulation error in the lower right subgraph of Figure 10. The predicted values of HA and ARIMA had large errors with the true values, and they lacked accuracy in fitting the peaks. The method based on deep learning was much better than the traditional method. HSTNet's overall fitting effect on traffic was higher than the other three. Especially during peak hours of network traffic, HSTNet achieved more accurate predictions. Compared to STDenseNet, its overall error in this area decreased by nearly 10% because HSTNet had better spatiotemporal feature extraction capabilities.

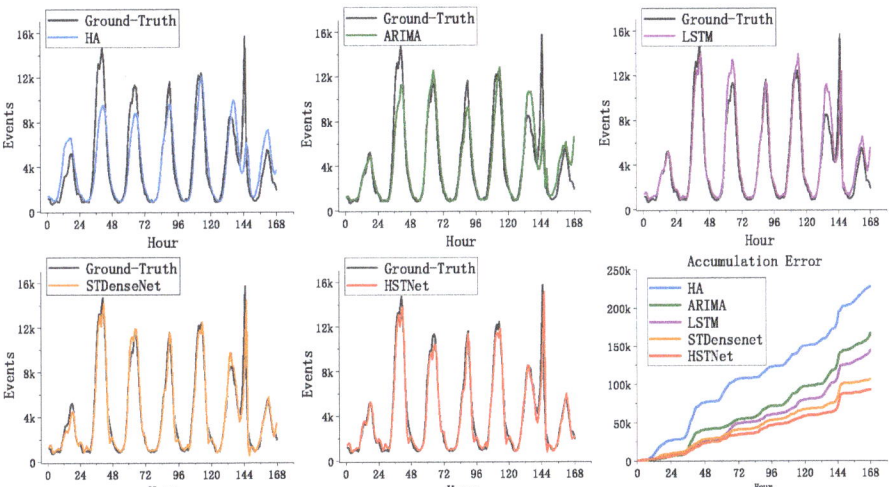

Figure 10. Comparison of the baseline and HSTNet on cell (50,58).

4.3. Experimental Result

In this part, we use HSTNet to predict the dataset and analyze the results. To verify the predictive performance of our model, we compared the predicted and actual values of the city's total traffic over one week and performed error analysis.

As shown in Figure 11, the X-axis represents the time interval in hours, and the Y-axis represents the total traffic for the entire city at the current time. Even for the difficult task of predicting overall urban traffic, the model still had a good fitting effect. A sharp rise in traffic was observed at 145 h in the figure due to the large error caused by the 2013 New Year's Eve event. The ability of the model to fit the traffic fluctuations caused by unexpected events needs to be improved.

HSTNet had the best prediction effect on the Call dataset. From the top right subgraph of Figure 11, it can be seen that the error value could be controlled within a certain range except for the impact caused by the unexpected event. The prediction effect of Internet traffic at night was not very satisfactory. There was a significant error in traffic prediction during this period, as shown in the lower right subgraph, because the three types of traffic had different scales of change. The Internet's day-night traffic gap was approximately two million (SMS and Call were only approximately 500 k), which created considerable difficulties in forecasting.

HSTNet also had good predictive performance for traffic in different areas of the city. Figure 12 shows a comparison of the predicted and real images at 10 o'clock on 24 December 2013. Each image had 100 × 100 cells. The brightness of the cell pixels indicates the traffic load of the corresponding cell. The brighter area indicates greater traffic load. This proved that our model could accurately predict the regions with different traffic distributions and could extract the spatial correlation of urban cellular traffic.

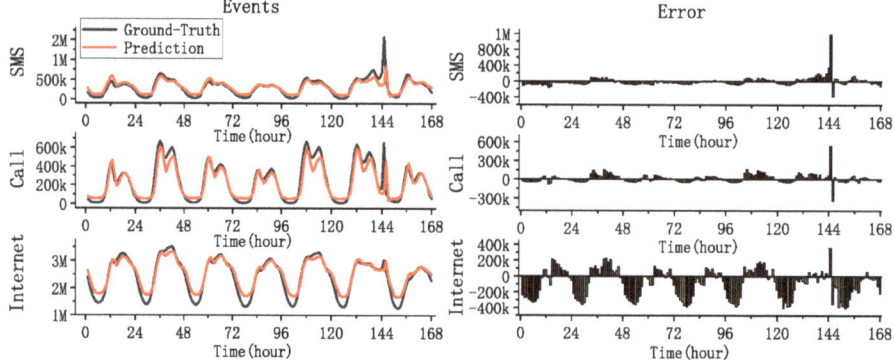

Figure 11. Comparison of hourly traffic prediction with the ground truth.

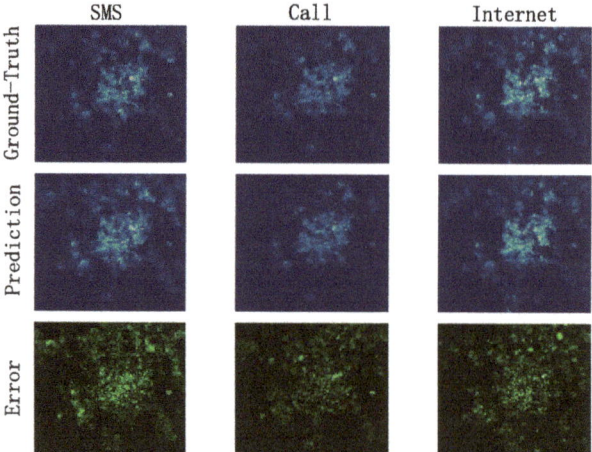

Figure 12. Comparison of predicted and real images.

The last line in Figure 12 shows the error between the corresponding prediction map and the ground truth. The brighter area indicates a greater error. We can see that the prediction error was not only biased towards the downtown area where the traffic load was large, but also, there were large errors in many suburbs with heavy traffic loads. This shows that the change in cellular traffic also depended on many factors that we had not considered, and a more sophisticated model is needed in the future to analyze the characteristics of cellular traffic changes.

5. Conclusions

This paper was devoted to the prediction of cellular network traffic. We conducted in-depth research on the spatiotemporal correlation of cellular networks and analyzed various factors that affect traffic changes, then proposed a hybrid deep learning model for traffic spatiotemporal prediction:

- This work used DenseNet with deformable convolution to extract the spatiotemporal characteristics of traffic.
- We introduced hour and holiday information to aid traffic forecasting.
- We proposed an attention module based on historical data to adjust the weight of the predicted traffic.

The experimental results showed that compared with the existing methods, the hybrid spatiotemporal network HSTNet proposed in this paper could better extract the spatiotemporal characteristics of image traffic data and improve the prediction accuracy, thus making more effective traffic prediction.

There are still many aspects that need improvement in our work:

- The model did not have a good ability to respond to fluctuations caused by emergencies.
- The forecast performance of the large scale traffic volume (total traffic volume of the entire city) needs to be improved.
- There are many external factors that we did not consider that could have a potential impact on cellular traffic changes.

In future work, traffic prediction modeling needs to consider not only the use of more sophisticated networks to extract features, but also the analysis and introduction of external data in multiple dimensions. It is worth mentioning that the introduction of our cellular traffic prediction scheme into traffic prediction problems in other similar contexts is also a very worthwhile research direction.

Author Contributions: Conceptualization, D.Z.; data curation, B.Y.; formal analysis, L.L.; funding acquisition, D.Z.; writing, original draft, D.Z. and L.L.; writing, review and editing, C.X. and Q.L. All authors have read and agreed to the published version of the manuscript.

Funding: This research was funded by the National Natural Science Foundation of China Grant Numbers 61402397, 61263043, 61562093, and 61663046.

Acknowledgments: This work is supported by: (i) the Natural Science Foundation China (NSFC) under Grant Nos. 61402397, 61263043, 61562093, and 61663046; (ii) Yunnan Provincial Young academic and technical leaders reserve talents under Grant No. 2017HB005; (iii) the Yunnan Provincial Innovation Team under Grant No. 2017HC012; and (iv) the Youth Talents Project of the China Association of Science and Technology under Grant No. W8193209.

Conflicts of Interest: The authors declare no conflict of interest.

References

1. Li, S.; Da Xu, L.; Zhao, S. 5G Internet of Things: A survey. *J. Ind. Inf. Integr.* **2018**, *10*, 1–9. [CrossRef]
2. Javaid, N.; Sher, A.; Nasir, H.; Guizani, N. Intelligence in IoT-based 5G networks: Opportunities and challenges. *IEEE Commun. Mag.* **2018**, *56*, 94–100. [CrossRef]
3. Wollschlaeger, M.; Sauter, T.; Jasperneite, J. The future of industrial communication: Automation networks in the era of the internet of things and industry 4.0. *IEEE Ind. Electron. Mag.* **2017**, *11*, 17–27. [CrossRef]
4. Akpakwu, G.A.; Silva, B.J.; Hancke, G.P.; Abu-Mahfouz, A.M. A survey on 5G networks for the Internet of Things: Communication technologies and challenges. *IEEE Access* **2017**, *6*, 3619–3647. [CrossRef]
5. Rao, S.K.; Prasad, R. Impact of 5G technologies on industry 4.0. *Wirel. Pers. Commun.* **2018**, *100*, 145–159. [CrossRef]
6. Huang, Y.; Tan, J.; Liang, Y.C. Wireless big data: Transforming heterogeneous networks to smart networks. *J. Commun. Inf. Netw.* **2017**, *2*, 19–32. [CrossRef]
7. Bi, S.; Zhang, R.; Ding, Z.; Cui, S. Wireless communications in the era of big data. *IEEE Commun. Mag.* **2015**, *53*, 190–199. [CrossRef]

8. Yao, C.; Yang, C.; Chih-Lin, I. Data-driven resource allocation with traffic load prediction. *J. Commun. Inf. Netw.* **2017**, *2*, 52–65. [CrossRef]
9. Shu, Y.; Yu, M.; Yang, O.; Liu, J.; Feng, H. Wireless traffic modeling and prediction using seasonal ARIMA models. *IEICE Trans. Commun.* **2005**, *88*, 3992–3999. [CrossRef]
10. Zhou, B.; He, D.; Sun, Z. Traffic predictability based on ARIMA/GARCH model. In Proceedings of the 2006 2nd Conference on Next Generation Internet Design and Engineering, Valencia, Spain, 3–5 April 2006.
11. Li, R.; Zhao, Z.; Zheng, J.; Mei, C.; Cai, Y.; Zhang, H. The learning and prediction of application-level traffic data in cellular networks. *IEEE Trans. Wirel. Commun.* **2017**, *16*, 3899–3912. [CrossRef]
12. Chen, X.; Jin, Y.; Qiang, S.; Hu, W.; Jiang, K. Analyzing and modeling spatio-temporal dependence of cellular traffic at city scale. In Proceedings of the 2015 IEEE International Conference on Communications (ICC), London, UK, 8–12 June 2015.
13. Wang, J.; Gong, B.; Liu, H.; Li, S. Multidisciplinary approaches to artificial swarm intelligence for heterogeneous computing and cloud scheduling. *Appl. Intell.* **2015**, *43*, 662–675. [CrossRef]
14. Sun, H.; Liu, H.X.; Xiao, H.; He, R.R.; Ran, B. Use of local linear regression model for short-term traffic forecasting. *Transp. Res. Rec.* **2003**, *1836*, 143–150. [CrossRef]
15. Sapankevych, N.I.; Sankar, R. Time series prediction using support vector machines: A survey. *IEEE Comput. Intell. Mag.* **2009**, *4*, 24–38. [CrossRef]
16. Wang, J.; Tang, J.; Xu, Z.; Wang, Y.; Xue, G.; Zhang, X.; Yang, D. Spatiotemporal modeling and prediction in cellular networks: A big data enabled deep learning approach. In Proceedings of the IEEE INFOCOM 2017—IEEE Conference on Computer Communications, Atlanta, GA, USA, 1–4 May 2017.
17. Zhang, C.; Zhang, H.; Yuan, D.; Zhang, M. Citywide cellular traffic prediction based on densely connected convolutional neural networks. *IEEE Commun. Lett.* **2018**, *22*, 1656–1659. [CrossRef]
18. Barlacchi, G.; De Nadai, M.; Larcher, R.; Casella, A.; Chitic, C.; Torrisi, G.; Antonelli, F.; Vespignani, A.; Pentland, A.; Lepri, B. A multi-source dataset of urban life in the city of Milan and the Province of Trentino. *Sci. Data* **2015**, *2*, 150055. [CrossRef] [PubMed]
19. Huang, G.; Liu, Z.; Van Der Maaten, L.; Weinberger, K.Q. Densely connected convolutional networks. In Proceedings of the IEEE Conference on Computer Vision and Pattern Recognition, Honolulu, HI, USA, 21–26 July 2017.
20. Dai, J.; Qi, H.; Xiong, Y.; Li, Y.; Zhang, G.; Hu, H.; Wei, Y. Deformable convolutional networks. In Proceedings of the IEEE International Conference on Computer Vision, Venice, Italy, 22–29 October 2017.
21. He, K.; Zhang, X.; Ren, S.; Sun, J. Deep residual learning for image recognition. In Proceedings of the IEEE Conference on Computer Vision and Pattern Recognition, Honolulu, HI, USA, 21–26 July 2017.
22. Kingma, D.P.; Ba, J. Adam: A method for stochastic optimization. *arXiv* **2014**, arXiv:1412.6980.

© 2020 by the authors. Licensee MDPI, Basel, Switzerland. This article is an open access article distributed under the terms and conditions of the Creative Commons Attribution (CC BY) license (http://creativecommons.org/licenses/by/4.0/).

MDPI
St. Alban-Anlage 66
4052 Basel
Switzerland
Tel. +41 61 683 77 34
Fax +41 61 302 89 18
www.mdpi.com

Algorithms Editorial Office
E-mail: algorithms@mdpi.com
www.mdpi.com/journal/algorithms

www.ingramcontent.com/pod-product-compliance
Lightning Source LLC
LaVergne TN
LVHW070547100526
838202LV00012B/401